HEADWAY

ELEMENTARY
PRONUNCIATIO

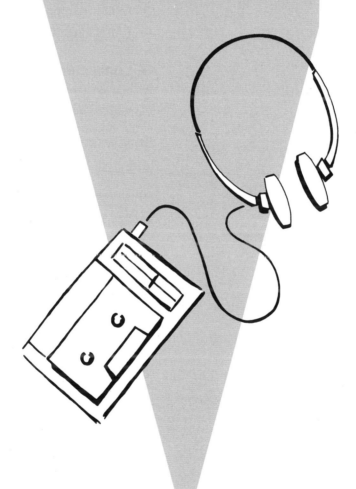

Sarah Cunningham   Peter Moor

Oxford University Press 1996

CONTENTS

* These exercises require reference to *Headway Elementary Student's Book,* page numbers of which are given. All other exercises can be done without reference to the Student's Book.

INTRODUCTION

To the student

● Welcome to *Headway Elementary Pronunciation*!

The questions and answers on these pages are to help you to understand this book, so that you can get the best out of it when you use it.

● Who is this book for?

Headway Elementary Pronunciation is for elementary students who want an introduction to English pronunciation.

Elementary students following other courses can easily use most of the exercises in *Headway Elementary Pronunciation*.

● How does this book work?

You can use this book (and tape) on their own. The exercises in it will help you to organize your study of pronunciation.

It is also part of the *Headway* course. Each of the fifteen units in this book links with one of the fifteen units of *Headway Elementary*.

● What types of exercise are there?

There are four different types of exercise in this book:

1   **Sounds** The connection between English spelling and pronunciation is often a problem for students of all nationalities. For this reason it is important to know the English sound symbols (phonemic symbols). These symbols help you to learn the pronunciation of new words easily.

Some Sounds exercises help you to learn the phonemic symbols. As you learn them, you write an example word under each symbol from the list given under the Phonemic symbols chart on page 50. These words help you to remember the sound symbols correctly.

Some Sounds exercises help with sounds that are a problem for speakers of only some languages. We show the languages like this:

(**D**) German   (**Gr**) Greek   (**J**) Japanese
(**E**) Spanish   (**H**) Hungarian   (**P**) Portuguese
(**F**) French   (**I**) Italian   (**Tr**) Turkish

Some exercises are useful for all nationalities. We show these like this:
(**All Nationalities**)

2   **Connected speech** These exercises help you to pronounce words in phrases and sentences correctly.

3   **Intonation and sentence stress** These exercises help you to hear and practise different kinds of intonation and sentence stress patterns.

4   **Word focus** In these exercises you study groups of words where there are problems with sounds and word stress.

● What's the connection with the *Headway* Student's Book?

The exercises in this book continue the vocabulary, grammar, and functional language work you do in the *Headway Elementary Student's Book*.

In this way, you can work on your pronunciation and revise vocabulary, grammar, and functional language at the same time.

Sometimes there is a connection with the Reading and Listening texts in the Student's Book too.

We show the connections with the Student's Book in the Contents Pages of this book.

● What about the tape?

This book comes with one tape.

Some exercises have different sections of tape (A, B, C, etc.).

The symbol in the exercise shows exactly which part of the tape you listen to.

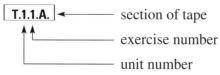

● What about the key?

The answers to exercises, and tapescripts which are not in the exercises themselves, are in the key at the back of the book.

As in the *Headway* Student's Book, sometimes we ask you questions to help you work out rules for yourself. The answers to these questions are in the key too.

The key symbol after an exercise means look at the key. The page number with the key symbol shows you exactly where to look:

⚷ p. 51

● What about technical words?

Here is a list of technical words we use in this book.

Use a bilingual dictionary to translate them.

You can look back at this list while you use the book.

consonant _____

contraction _____

flat _____

intonation _____

linking _____

phonemic _____

polite _____

pronunciation _____

rude _____

sentence _____

sound _____

spelling _____

stress _____

syllable _____

symbol _____

vowel _____

UNIT 1

● Sounds

1 Introduction to consonant sounds

| T.1.1.A. | Listen and look at the spelling.

/k/ → cake   /keɪk/
     → chemist's /kemɪsts/

| T.1.1.B. | Look at the spelling and listen to these words.

c → /k/ cassette   /kəset/
  → /s/ cigarette /sɪgəret/

The **sound** and the **spelling** are not always the same in English. To find the pronunciation of new words, look at the phonemic symbols in your dictionary.

chemist (/ˈkemɪst/) n. farmacista m./f.; (scientist) chimico, a m., f. ~ry n. chimica f.

It is important to learn the phonemic symbols.

Easy consonant symbols

☐	/p/	**p**en	☐	/s/	**s**ister
☐	/b/	**b**ag	☐	/z/	Bra**z**il
☐	/t/	**t**icke**t**	☐	/l/	**l**etter
☐	/d/	**d**ictionary	☐	/m/	**m**agazine
☐	/k/	**c**lock	☐	/n/	**n**ame
☐	/g/	**G**reece	☐	/h/	**h**ello
☐	/f/	**f**amily	☐	/r/	**R**ussia
☐	/v/	**v**an	☐	/w/	**w**ant

1 | T.1.1.C. | Listen and tick (✓) the consonant sounds that are the same in your language.

2 Which sounds are very different in your language? Are there any sounds that you don't have? Discuss your answers with your teacher.

3 Look at the phonemic symbols on page 50. Find the words from the box for sounds 1–16. Write them in the spaces under the symbols.

You will learn the other consonant symbols as you work through the book.

● Word focus

2 The sound of English

1 | T.1.2.A. | Look at the pictures below and on the next page. Listen to the words in three different languages. Which is English? Tick a, b or c.

1.    a ☐   b ✓   c ☐

2.    a ☐   b ☐   c ☐

3.    a ☐   b ☐   c ☐

1

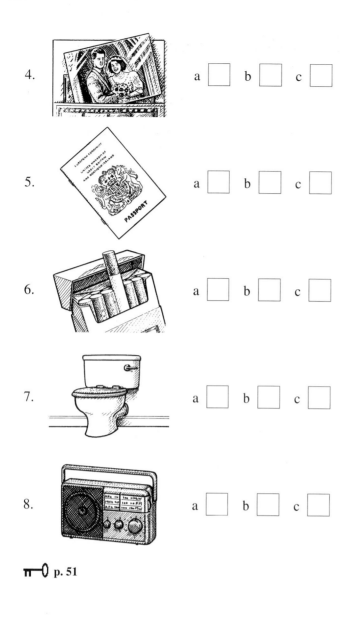

4. a ☐ b ☐ c ☐

5. a ☐ b ☐ c ☐

6. a ☐ b ☐ c ☐

7. a ☐ b ☐ c ☐

8. a ☐ b ☐ c ☐

⚷ p. 51

2 **T.1.2.B.** Listen to the English words again and practise saying them.

3 Look at the stress.

● telephone   ● cassette   ● television

Listen again and mark the stress on the words below.

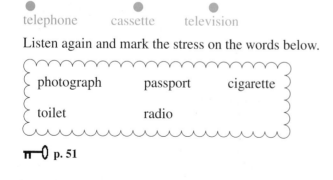

photograph   passport   cigarette

toilet   radio

⚷ p. 51

To find where the stress is on a new word, you can look at the stress mark in your dictionary.

> **telephon|e** /ˈtelɪfəʊn/ n teléfono m. —vt llamar por teléfono. ~**e booth** n cabina f telefónica. ~**e directory** n guía f telefónica. ~**e exchange** n central f telefónica. ~**ic** /ˈfɒnɪk/ a telefónico. ~**ist** /tɪˈlefənɪst/ n telefonista m & f

Practise saying the words with the correct stress.

---

3 Stress in numbers

1 **T.1.3.A.** Listen to the stress in these numbers.

13	○ ● thirteen	● ○ thirty	**30**
14	fourteen	forty	**40**
15	fifteen	fifty	**50**
16	sixteen	sixty	**60**
17	seventeen	seventy	**70**
18	eighteen	eighty	**80**
19	nineteen	ninety	**90**

Listen again and practise saying the numbers with the correct stress.

2 **T.1.3.B.** Choose one of the cards below, a, b or c. Listen and cross out (✗) the numbers that you hear. You will hear each number twice. Who finishes first: a, b or c?

a

13	60	14
50	70	15
90	18	19

b

80	16	90
15	30	14
18	17	19

c

90	13	50
14	17	16
19	40	80

⚷ p. 51

3 Make a new card. You choose the numbers. Play the game again. Your teacher or another student will read out some numbers. They will be in a different order from the numbers on the tape. When you finish your card, shout *Bingo!*

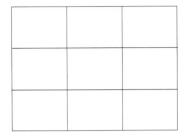

Connected speech

4 Short forms (contractions) of *be*

1 **T.1.4.A.** Look at the short forms of *be* below.

I'm (= I am)
you're (= you are)
he's (= he is)
she's (= she is)
it's (= it is)
that's (= that is)
my name's (= my name is)

Listen and practise.

2 Jane is talking about her pets. Circle where the short forms go – there are seven more.

T.1.4.B. Listen and check your answers.

🔑 p. 51

Practise reading what Jane says, using short forms.

3 Think about your pet or an animal you know. Complete the information below.

Animal's name: _____

Animal's age: _____

Intelligent/Stupid: _____

Tell the other students about your pet. Use contractions!

I'm

Hello. (I am) Jane. This is my cat. Her name is Pepper. She is three years old and she is very intelligent, I think!

That is my dog, Sam. Sam is twelve years old now! He is a very nice dog, but he is very stupid!

UNIT 2

● Sounds

1 Problem consonants: / r /

(All Nationalities)

1   **T.2.1.**   Listen to the sound / r /. Is it the same in your language?

Rolls Royce

The River Rhine

Right and Wrong

Rock 'n' Roll

a red, red rose

Look.

/ r /

Listen again and practise saying the phrases.

2 Silent 'r'

(All Nationalities)

Look.

child**r**en	= letter *r* + vowel sound	= / r /
su**r**name	= letter *r* + consonant sound	= ✗
mothe**r**	= letter *r* + nothing	= ✗

⚠️   are   = / ɑ: /
      aren't = / ɑ:nt /
      The *e* is silent.

1   **T.2.2.A.**   Listen to these examples.

r + vowel sound	*r* + consonant sound or nothing
boyf**r**iend	siste**r**
G**r**anny	fathe**r**
ma**rr**ied	first name

Practise saying the words and phrases.

2   Cross out (✗) the *r*s that are not pronounced in the words below.

hai~~r~~dresse~~r~~	**nurse**
engineer	doctor
	director
artist	**interpreter**
receptionist	*writer*

T.2.2.B.   Listen and check your answers.
🔑 p. 51

Practise saying the words.

3 Look at the Reading text on page 16 of the Student's Book. Find seven *r*s that are pronounced, and seven *r*s that are **not** pronounced.

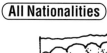 p. 51

> The rules for silent *r* are only for British English. In American English all *r*s are pronounced.

---

3 The sound / ə /

(**All Nationalities**)

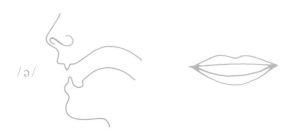

1 **T.2.3.A.** Are these food words the same in your language? Listen to the pronunciation in English.

One sound is very important – the sound / ə /.

/ə/
Example hamburger

This is the most frequent vowel sound in English. It is in weak or unstressed syllables. You make it like this.

/ə/

2 Listen again and mark the / ə / sounds and stress like this.

● /ə/
hamburger

 p. 51

Listen again and practise saying the words.

3 Match the words to the pictures.

a	potato	3	f	orange	___
b	pepper	___	g	banana	___
c	yoghurt	___	h	chocolate	___
d	chicken	___	i	coffee	___
e	tuna	___	j	sandwich	___

1 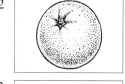 6

2 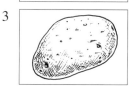 7

3  8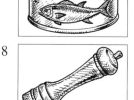

4  9

5

10

p. 51

4 **T.2.3.B.** Listen and tick the words that have an / ə / sound.

p. 51

5 Listen again and mark the stress.

p. 51

Practise saying the words.

● Stress

4 Introduction to sentence stress

1 **T.2.4.A.** The computer is asking Jack some questions. Listen.

In Jack's answers some words are strong and some words are weak. The important words are strong. The others are weak.

☐ ■
My name's Jack.

⚠ It is important to use strong and weak words like Jack, or you will sound like the computer!

2 Practise Jack's answers, like this.

	☐ ■
mm MM MM	My name's Jack.
	■
mm mm MM	I'm from Leeds.
	■
mm mm mm-MM-mm	I'm a mechanic.
	■
mm MM-mm	I'm twenty.
	☐ ■
MM mm MM	No, I'm not.

3 **T.2.4.B.** Look at the computer's questions. Which are the important (strong) words? Listen to a real person asking the questions and mark the strong words.

☐ ■
Example What's your name?
π─O p. 51

π─O p. 51

4 Listen again and practise the questions. Then practise the questions and answers with a partner.

UNIT 3

● Sounds

1 Problem consonants: final '-s'

(All Nationalities)

A lot of words end in -s in English.

<table>
<tr><td>a Plural nouns

cups /s/
pens
stamps</td><td>b he/she
Present Simple forms
speaks
reads
likes</td></tr>
<tr><td>c Possessives
Anna's friend
Jane's bag
Pete's mum</td><td>d Contraction of is
It's here.
How's Andy?
He's okay.</td></tr>
</table>

 The final -s is **always** pronounced in English.

Sometimes the sound is / s /.

Example   / s / cups

Sometimes the sound is / z /.

Example   / z / pens

1 ☐ **T.3.1.** Listen to the words and phrases above. Write in the pronunciation of -s : / s / or / z /.

🔑 **p. 51**

Listen again and practise saying the words.

2 Final '-es' pronounced / ɪz /

(All Nationalities)

The final -es is pronounced / ɪz / after:

-s or -ss / s /	-sh / ʃ /	-ch / tʃ /
kisses	washes	matches
buses	pushes	churches

-x / ks /	-z / z /	-ge / dʒ /
boxes	Liz's	pages
mixes	houses*	oranges

⚠ ***Note**   house = / haʊs /
houses = / haʊzɪz /

1 ☐ **T.3.2.** Listen and practise saying the words above.

2 Work with a partner.

Student A Look at card **A** on p. 8.
Student B Look at card **B** on p. 9.

Read each word to your partner. Your partner must say the word with -s at the end (pronounced / z / or / ɪz /).

You can check the answers at the bottom of the card.

7

● Connected speech

3 Weak forms and linking

1   Match the word in **A** to the opposite in **B**.

A	B
get up	finish
open	leave
arrive	go to bed
start	close

🔑 p. 51

2   **T.3.3.A.** Listen and count the words you hear.
(*o'clock* = one word)

a `6`   _____ bank opens _____ .

b ☐   He goes _____ seven _____ .

c ☐   This office _____ half past two.

d ☐   We get up _____ o'clock.

e ☐   Her plane _____ two fifteen.

f ☐   The programme _____ about

_____ thirty.

g ☐   The film _____ at half _____

_____ .

h ☐   My train _____ about _____

_____ .

🔑 p. 51

3   Listen again and write in the missing words.

🔑 p. 51

4   When we speak fast, we make some words weak. The
weak words often have the sound /ə/.

/ə/   /ə/
at nine o'clock

The weak words are not stressed.

T.3.3.B. Practise saying these times. Use the
weak forms.

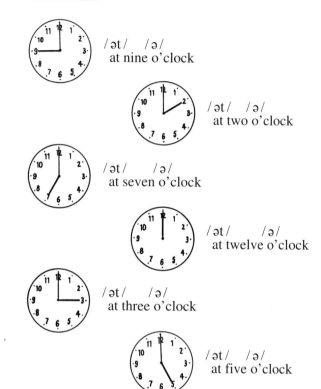

/ət/   /ə/
at nine o'clock

/ət/   /ə/
at two o'clock

/ət/   /ə/
at seven o'clock

/ət/   /ə/
at twelve o'clock

/ət/   /ə/
at three o'clock

/ət/   /ə/
at five o'clock

5   When we speak fast, we also link words together. We
do this when one word ends with a consonant sound
and the next word begins with a vowel sound.

The bank opens at nine o'clock.

Here are some more examples. Practise saying them.

He goes to bed at seven o'clock.

This office closes at half past two.

We get up at about eight o'clock.

6   Look at sentences e–h in 2 above. Find the words that
link together.

🔑 p. 51

Practise saying all the sentences. Speak fast, using
weak forms and linking.

● Intonation

4 Introduction to intonation: up or down?

1 | **T.3.4.** | Listen to the pairs of words below. One is a question. Write **.** next to the statements, and **?** next to the questions.

a	Okay	**.**	Okay	**?**
b	Bill		Bill	
c	Yes		Yes	
d	Coffee		Coffee	

 p. 52

2 We know these words are questions because the intonation goes **up**.

Okay?

The other words are **not** questions. The intonation goes down.

Okay.

Is this the same in your language?

Listen again and repeat. Pay attention to the up and down intonation.

3 Work with a partner. Say the words below. Sometimes use question intonation (■⤴) and sometimes use statement intonation (■⤵). Your partner must say if you are asking a question.

Example

~~~~~~~~~~~~~~~~~~~~~~~~
| Milk | Here | Really |
| No | Sorry* | Anne | Ready |
~~~~~~~~~~~~~~~~~~~~~~~~

Sorry? as a question = Say it again.

UNIT 4

● Sounds

1 Introduction to vowel sounds (1)

There are twelve vowel sounds in English.
Here are six of them.

/iː/	see	/uː/	two
/ɪ/	is	/e/	yes
/ʊ/	good	/ə/	the

1 ┃ **T.4.1.A.** ┃ Listen and answer the questions.

  a Which sounds are long?

  b Which are the same (or very similar) in your language?

  c Which ones don't you have in your language?

π–◯ **p. 52**

Listen again and practise.

2 ┃ **T.4.1.B.** ┃ Listen to the verbs and write in the symbol for the vowel sound(s).

    / /
a sp<u>ea</u>k

    / /
b sp<u>e</u>ll

    / /
c l<u>i</u>ve

    / // /
d l<u>i</u>st<u>e</u>n

    / /
e l<u>oo</u>k

    / /
f d<u>o</u>

    / /
g l<u>ea</u>ve

    / /
h c<u>oo</u>k

π–◯ **p. 52**

Listen again and practise saying the verbs.

3 Look at the phonemic symbols on page 50. Find the words from the box for sounds 25, 26, 27, 32, 33, and 36. Write them in the spaces under the symbols.

You will learn the other vowel symbols in Unit 5.

● Stress and connected speech

2 Weak forms in Present Simple questions

1 ┃ **T.4.2.A.** ┃ Listen to the dialogues and write in **B**'s answers.

a

b

c

d

e

f

π—○ p. 52

In fast speech *Do you* is often pronounced /dʒə/.

/dʒə/
Do you know the time?

/dʒə/
Do you have a light?

/dʒə/
Do you speak English?

2　[T.4.2.B.]　Practise the questions. Start with the strong words, like this.

　　　　　　□　■
　　　　know the time?

　　/jə/　□　■
　　you　know the time?

　/dʒə/　□　■
　Do you know the time?

3　Practise the other questions in the same way. Practise the dialogues with a partner. Pronounce *Do you* correctly.

4　Look at the questions below. Check the meaning of new words in your dictionary or with your teacher. Practise saying the questions, pronouncing *Do you* correctly.

> **a** Where do you live?
>
> **b** Do you live with your parents?
>
> **c** Do you have any children?
>
> **d** Do you like learning English?
>
> **e** Do you study English a lot at home?
>
> **f** Do you speak other languages?
>
> **g** What do you do at the weekend/in your spare time?
>
> **h** Do you smoke?
>
> **i** Do you like .... ?*
>
> **j** What sort of music/books/films do you like?
>
> * person/place/food/actor/rock group/hobby etc.

5　Choose five of these questions. Decide **who** you want to ask. All stand up and ask each other.

3 Weak forms of *a* and *the*

1 Margaret is talking to her new colleague, Shirley, about her family. You can see their conversation below, but the words *a* and *the* are not there. Read the conversation, and put in eight *a*s and two *the*s. The first two are done for you.

M Do you have children, Shirley?

S Yes, <u>a</u> son and <u>a</u> daughter.

M Oh, that's nice, what do they do?

S My daughter Jenny's music teacher, and Michael, my son, is at college – he wants to be pilot!

M Oh, lovely!

S Yes …

M Do they live at home?

S Michael lives with me, but Jenny lives in London – she's married with two children.

M Oh! So you're grandmother!

S Yes, she has girl and boy too – Rebecca and Thomas.

M Oh, lovely – how old are they?

S girl's seven and boy's two – do you want to see photo?

M Oh yes. … Ah … aren't they beautiful!

T.4.3.A. Listen and check your answers.
🎧 p. 52

2 *a* and *the* are nearly always pronounced as **weak** forms. They have the vowel sound /ə/.

/ə/	/ðə/
a girl	the girl

/ə/	/ðə/
a boy	the boy

T.4.3.B. Practise saying the phrases below. Pronounce *a* and *the* correctly.

a a girl   a boy
  a daughter   a son
  She's a music teacher. He wants to be a pilot.

b the girl   the boy
  the daughter   the son

3 Look at the dialogue again. Some words are strong (stressed).

Do you **have children**, Shirley?

Yes, a **son** and a **daughter**.

These are the important words.

Practise saying the dialogue line by line. Pay attention to the stress, and the pronunciation of *a* and *the*. Read the dialogue aloud with a partner.

4 Work in pairs. Have a similar conversation about your families. Pay attention to the pronunciation of *a* and *the*.

● Word focus

4 How many syllables?

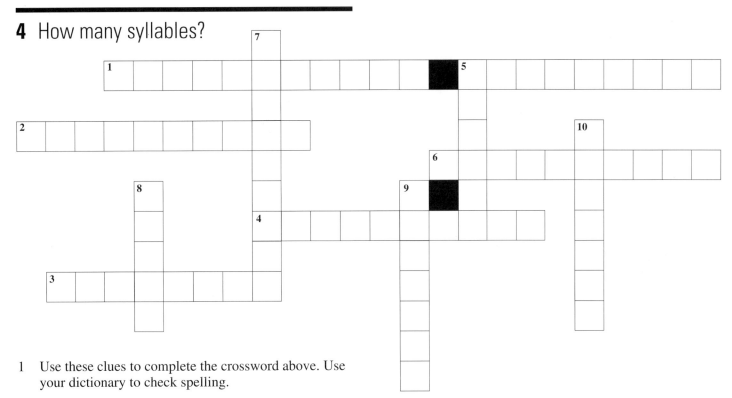

1 Use these clues to complete the crossword above. Use your dictionary to check spelling.

Across
1 the opposite of boring
2 You can buy lunch or dinner here.
3 the month after January
4 You use it to find the meaning of new words.
5 brown and sweet, children love it
6 potatoes, carrots, peas, cabbage

Down
5 You use it to take photos.
7 the day before Thursday
8 all, each
9 military man
10 not single – has a husband/wife

> **T.4.4.** Listen and check your answers.
> π–0 p. 52

2 In English, some words have 'silent syllables'.

interesting = /ˈɪn|trəs|tɪŋ/ = three syllables

Write the words from the crossword on a piece of paper. How many syllables are there in each word? Listen again and check.

π–0 p. 52

3 Which syllable is silent? Cross out the 'silent syllables' and mark the stress like this.

●
intᗱresting
π–0 p. 52

Practise saying the words. Don't put in any extra syllables!

4 Here are some more words with 'silent syllables'. How many syllables are there in each word?

> a aren't   d comfortable
> b evening   e family
> c favourite   f secretary

π–0 p. 52

Practise saying the words.

5 Practise saying the phrases below.

my favourite chocolate

every Wednesday evening

What an interesting camera!

Are you comfortable?

They aren't married.

UNIT 5

● Sounds

1 Introduction to vowel sounds (2)

1 **T.5.1.A.** Listen to the other six vowel sounds.

/ɜ:/ word *curtain*

/ɔ:/ four _____

/æ/ man _____

/ʌ/ bus _____

/ɑ:/ part _____

/ɒ/ shop _____

Practise saying the sounds. Cover the words. Can you remember the word for each sound?

2 **T.5.1.B.** Listen to the vowel sounds in the words below.

carpet

cup

lamp

pots

wall

curtain

Write the words next to the correct symbol in 1.

⊓─O p. 52

14

3 Below are some more 'home' words. Look at the phonemic symbols. Match them with the pictures below. Write the word on the line.

a /frɪdʒ/ **8**   f /mɪrə/

b /dɔ:/   g /kʊkə/

c /gɑ:dən/   h /lɪvɪŋ ru:m/

d /bɑ:θ/   i /telɪvɪʒən/

e /kʌbəd/   j /wɒʃɪŋ məʃi:n/

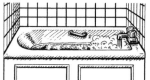

1. _____

6. _____

2. _____

7. _____

3. _____

8. *fridge*

4. _____

9. _____

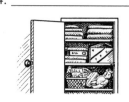

5. _____

10. _____

4 **T.5.1.C.** Listen and check your answers.

🔑 p. 52

Practise saying the words, paying attention to the pronunciation of the vowel sounds.

5 Look at the phonemic symbols on page 50. Find the words from the box for sounds 28, 29, 30, 31, 34, and 35. Write them in the spaces under the symbols.

2 Problem consonants: / θ / and / ð / ('th')

(All Nationalities)

1 **T.5.2.A.** Listen. A lot of English words are spelt with *th*. These letters are pronounced / θ / or / ð /.

/ θ /	/ ð /
three	this
thirty	that
thousand	these
thin	those
theatre	there

To make these sounds, the tongue must touch the back of your teeth like this.

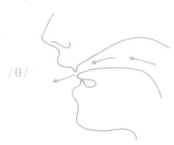

/ θ /

If you have problems with the sounds, put your finger in front of your mouth and touch it with your tongue, like this.

⚠️ With the sound / ð / you use your voice. With / θ / you do not use your voice.

Listen again and practise saying the words.

2 Work in groups of three.

Look at Unit 5 of the Student's Book. Find eight words spelt with *th* (not the words above). Are they pronounced / θ / or / ð /? Use your dictionary to check.

The first group to finish shouts *Stop!* The winning group reads out their answers. If they pronounce a word incorrectly, the other groups can shout *Challenge!*

3 **T.5.2.B.** Look at the pictures and listen.

 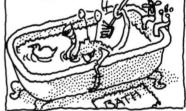

a This is a Thing.   b This is a Thing having a bath.

c This is a Thing with his three brothers.

d Three Things together at the theatre

e This Thing's thirtieth birthday

Read the sentences. Pay attention to the *th* sounds!

4 Look at the phonemic symbols on page 50. Find the words from the box for sounds 18 and 19. Write them in the spaces under the symbols.

● Intonation

3 Sounding polite

1 | **T.5.3.A.** | Listen to the people in office A and the
people in office B.

Why do the people in Office B **sound** more friendly?
Do you use intonation like this in your language? Do
you think it is important?

2   In English it is very important to use intonation to
sound polite and friendly. Look at the difference
between the voices in Office A and Office B.

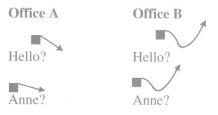

Office A   Office B

Hello?   Hello?

Anne?   Anne?

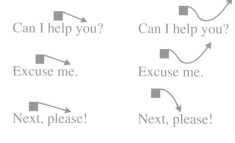

Can I help you?   Can I help you?

Excuse me.   Excuse me.

Next, please!   Next, please!

Listen again and practise the polite, friendly intonation
of Office B.

3 Look at the picture of the Tourist Information Office.
Below the picture are the lines of three conversations.
Write the lines in the correct speech bubble.

Desk 1

Yes, please. Is the Museum of Modern Art near here?

Hello. Can I help you?

Mmm, just a minute … here's a map …

Desk 2

Sorry, we don't have information about hotels. Try
next door.

Next, please.

Hello, can you help me? I want a hotel for three nights.

Thank you.

Desk 3

Sure, on the left opposite the underground station.

Yes, sir?

Excuse me …

Is there a bookshop near here?

T.5.3.B. Listen and check your answers.
p. 52

4 Practise saying the dialogues line by line. Copy the
polite intonation. Practise the dialogues with a partner.

UNIT 6

● Sounds

1 Problem consonants: / w /

All Nationalities

1 | **T.6.1.A.** | Listen to the sentences. Underline the / w / sounds.

a

c

b

d

🔑 p. 52

2 Do you have the sound / w / in your language?

The sound / w / is made like this.

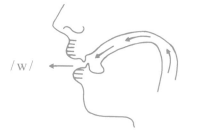

/ w /

Try starting with / uː /.

uuu … where	uuu … was
uu … where	uu … was
u … where	u … was
where	was

3 Practise saying the sentences in 1. Start very slowly, then say them faster and faster.

4 | **T.6.1.B.** | Listen to the pairs of words below. Can you hear the difference?

A	B
good	wood
gun	won
veal	wheel
vet	wet

Practise saying the pairs of words.

2 Silent 'w'

All Nationalities

1 Match the words in the box with the phonemic symbols below.

when *i*	who	swim	what
week *h*	winter	whole	twenty
wrong	we	two	write

a / wiː /	e / rɒŋ /	i / wen /
b / tuː /	f / raɪt /	j / swɪm /
c / huː /	g / ˈtwentɪ /	k / həʊl /
d / ˈwɪntə /	h / wiːk /	l / wɒt /

🔑 p. 52

2 Find five words in the box with a silent *w*. Underline them.

🔑 p. 53

18

3 Find another example in the box to complete the rules below.

Rule	Examples
a *w* before *r* is silent.	write, _____
b *wh* and *o:* w is silent.	who, _____

🔑 p. 53

4 | T.6.2. | Listen and practise saying the silent *w* words.

● Connected speech

3 Pronunciation of negative forms

1 | T.6.3.A. | Listen to the dialogue. Do not write in the verbs. Tick (✓) the affirmative verbs, and cross (✗) the negatives.

Bob My mother's parents, Thomas and Frida

_____ (a ✓) a strange couple.

They _____ (b ☐) married nearly sixty

years. They _____ (c ☐) very rich, but they

_____ (d ☐) very happy.

Jack Why?

Bob Frida _____ (e ☐) English ... she

_____ (f ☐) speak English very well.

Jack Where _____ (g ☐) she from?

Bob Berlin ... Germany.

Jack _____ (h ☐) Thomas speak German?

Bob Well, he _____ (i ☐) speak many

languages, but he _____ (j ☐) speak

German.

Jack That's strange! And what about your mother?

_____ (k ☐) she speak German?

Bob Well, she _____ (l ☐) understand it very

well, but she _____ (m ☐) really speak it.

🔑 p. 53

2 Listen again and fill in the correct verb form:
was/wasn't; were/weren't; can/can't; could/couldn't.

🔑 p. 53

3 When we speak fast, we use contractions and weak forms for these verbs.

| T.6.3.B. | Listen and practise.

a was = / wəz /
Where was she from?

b wasn't = / wɒznt /
She wasn't English.

c were = / wə /
They were very rich.

d weren't = / wɜ:nt /
They weren't very happy.

e can = / kən /
She can understand it.

f can't = / kɑ:nt /
She can't speak it.

g could = / kəd /
He could speak many languages.

h couldn't = / kʊ(d)nt /
He couldn't speak German.

4 Practise saying the dialogue line by line, paying attention to the pronunciation of these verb forms. Practise the dialogue with a partner.

UNIT 7

● Sounds

1 Problem vowel sounds: / ɪ / and / iː /
Ⓔ Ⓕ Ⓖⓡ Ⓗ Ⓘ Ⓟ Ⓣⓡ

1 Look at the words below. Check the meaning of new words in your dictionary or with your teacher.

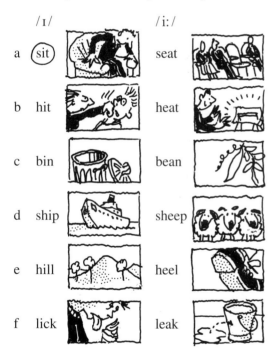

	/ ɪ /	/ iː /
a	(sit)	seat
b	hit	heat
c	bin	bean
d	ship	sheep
e	hill	heel
f	lick	leak

2 **T.7.1.A.** Listen and circle the word you hear twice.
 p. 53

3 / ɪ / is a **short** sound. To make it your lips look like this.

/ ɪ /

/iː/ is a **long** sound. To make it your lips look like this.

/iː/

Practise saying the pairs of words.

4 **T.7.1.B.** Look at the words below. Listen to the instructions on the tape and join the words with lines. You will make a letter of the alphabet. What is it?

eat •   • live   • cheap   • hit

•leave   • it   • wheel   • will

chip •   •heat   • fill   • feel

•hill   seat   sit   heel •
         •   •

bin •   ship •   bean •   • sheep

fit •   •   •   • lick
    feet   leak

 p. 53

20

● Word focus

2 Past Simple forms that are difficult to pronounce

1 Look at the verbs below. Check the meaning of new words in your dictionary or with your teacher. Write in the past form.

a read *read*

b learn _____

c run _____

d fall _____

e see _____

f hear _____

g buy _____

h say _____

i teach _____

j think _____

π—◯ p. 53

2 Can you pronounce the past forms?

You can find the pronunciation in your dictionary.

a
> **read** / riːd/ *verb* (**reads, reading, read**
> (red) **has read**)
> **1** look at words and understand them:
> *Have you read this book? It's very
> interesting.*

Look at the phonemic transcription of *read*. Can you pronounce it?

3 Can you pronounce the past forms below?

b
> **learn** /lɜːn/ *verb* (**learns, learning, learnt**
> (lɜːnt) **or learned** (lɜːnd) **has learnt or**
> **has learned**)
> **1** find out something, or how to do some-
> thing _____ by doing it often:

c
> **run**[1] /rʌn/ *verb* (**runs, running, ran** (ræn)
> **has run**)
> **1** move very quickly on your legs: *I was
> late so I ran to the bus-stop.*
> **2** go; make a journey: *The buses don't run
> on Sundays.*

d
> **fall**[1] /fɔːl/ *verb* (**falls, falling, fell** (fel)
> **has fallen** /'fɔːlən/)
> **1** go down quickly; drop: *The book fell off
> the table.* ◇ *She fell down the stairs and*

e
> **see** /siː/ *verb* (**sees, seeing, saw** (sɔː)
> **has seen** /siːn/)
> **1** know something using your eyes: *It was
> so dark _____ couldn't _____ anything*

f
> **hear** /hɪə(r)/ *verb* (**hears, hearing, heard**
> (hɜːd) **has heard**)
> **1** get sounds with your ears: *Can you hear
> that noise?* ◇ *I _____ somebody laughing*

T.7.2.A. Listen and check your answers. Practise saying the past forms.

4 Use your dictionary to find the pronunciation of the past forms of *buy*, *say*, *teach*, and *think*.

T.7.2.B. Listen and check your answers. Practise saying the past forms.

● Connected speech

3 Hearing Past Simple forms

T.7.3.A. *-ed* at the end of regular Past Simple forms is pronounced in three different ways. Listen.

/ t /	/ d /	/ ɪd /
liked	loved	hated
worked	lived	intended
finished	opened	started
stopped	arrived	ended

1 Practise saying the verbs in the three groups above.

2 Complete the rule.

> The *-ed* ending is pronounced / ɪd / if the infinitive
> of the verb ends with the sound /_____/ or /_____/.

π—◯ p. 53

3 **T.7.3.B.** In a sentence the *-ed* form is sometimes difficult to hear. Listen to the three pairs of sentences below. Can you hear the difference between a (Present Simple) and b (Past Simple)?

1. a We like her.
   b We liked her.

2. a I love him.
   b I loved him.

3. a They hate it.
   b They hated it.

Listen again and practise saying the pairs of sentences.

21

4 **T.7.3.C.** Listen to the sentences and circle the verb you hear, Present Simple or Past Simple.

a We *arrive/(arrived)* on Monday morning.

b It *opens/opened* at nine o'clock.

c I *finish/finished* work on Friday afternoon at six o'clock.

d They *close/closed* on Monday.

e They *start/started* at eight o'clock.

f The trains *stop/stopped* at midnight.

🔑 p. 53

5 **T.7.3.D.** Close your book. Listen and practise saying each sentence in the Past Simple. Pay attention to the pronunciation of the -ed ending.

● Stress and intonation

4 Intonation in *Wh-* questions

1 **T.7.4.A.** You will hear the *beginning* of seven questions. Listen and tick the correct words below to finish the questions. There is only **one** correct answer.

1. ☐ a … you born?
   ☐ b … did you born?
   ☑ c … were you born?

2. ☐ a … born your sister?
   ☐ b … your sister born?
   ☐ c … you born?

3. ☐ a … married?
   ☐ b … born?
   ☐ c … birthday?

4. ☐ a … her grandfather die?
   ☐ b … die her grandfather?
   ☐ c … her grandfather died?

5. ☐ a … was he?
   ☐ b … he was?
   ☐ c … he did?

6. ☐ a … went to university?
   ☐ b … were to university?
   ☐ c … go to university?

7. ☐ a … you leave university?
   ☐ b … you were left university?
   ☐ c … you left university?

2 **T.7.4.B.** Listen to the full questions and their replies. Check your answers.

🔑 p. 53

3 In *Wh-* questions (questions with *What, Who, When, Where, Why, How*, etc.) the intonation usually goes **down** on the main stress, not up.

Where were you born?

When was your sister born?

⚠ If your intonation is **flat** you may sound **rude**.

T.7.4.C. It helps to **start** the question quite **high**.

Where were you born?

Where were you born?

Where were you born?

Practise saying the other questions in the same way.

4 ◀ **T.7.4.B.** Work with a partner. Look at the tapescript on page 53. Practise reading the dialogues together.

UNIT 8

● Sounds

1 Problem consonants: /dʒ/
Ⓓ Ⓔ Ⓕ Ⓖⓡ Ⓟ Ⓣⓡ

1 ⬚ **T.8.1.** ⬚ Listen to the sound /dʒ/ in these names.

Do you have this sound in your language?

The sound /dʒ/ is made with the two sounds /d/ and /ʒ/ like this. First say /d/.

/d/

Then move your tongue down to say /ʒ/.

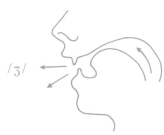

/ʒ/

Repeat each sound quickly until you say the two sounds together. You use your voice. Feel your throat vibrate when you say it.

Listen again and practise saying the names.

2 Below are some famous people with the sound /dʒ/ in their names. Who are they?

a /dʒɒn ˈlenən/ _____

b /mɪk ˈdʒægə/ _____

c /dʒæk ˈkenədɪ/ _____

d /ˈdʒænɪt ˈdʒæksən/ _____

e /ˈdʒuːlɪə ˈrɒbəts/ _____

f /dʒeɪn ˈfɒndə/ _____

⛝⃛〇 p. 53

Practise saying their names.

3 Look at the phonemic symbols on page 50. Find the word from the box for sound 23. Write it in the space under the symbol.

2 Problem vowel sounds: /ɜː/
Ⓓ Ⓔ Ⓖⓡ Ⓘ

1 ⬚ **T.8.2.A.** ⬚ Listen to the words below. They all have the sound /ɜː/.

work	**learn**	girl	**first**
	nurse	**world**	**third**
her	heard	*word*	

The vowel sound is spelt in many ways but all of the words have an *r*. Is the *r* pronounced?

⛝⃛〇 p. 53

23

2 ⬚ **T.8.2.B.** Listen to some longer words and underline the / ɜː / sound. Which three words don't have an / ɜː / sound?

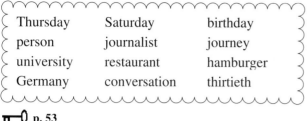

Thursday	Saturday	birthday
person	journalist	journey
university	restaurant	hamburger
Germany	conversation	thirtieth

π⊸ **p. 53**

3 The sound / ɜː / is made in the middle of the mouth. The lips are relaxed like this.

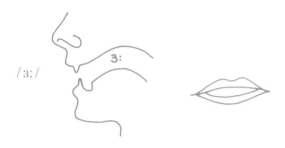

/ ɜː /

/ ɜː / is a **long** sound.

Listen again and practise saying the words in 1 and 2 above.

4 ⬚ **T.8.2.C.** Look at the newspaper headlines below. Check the meaning of new words in your dictionary or with your teacher. Listen to the headlines one by one. How many / ɜː / sounds are there? Write the number in the box.

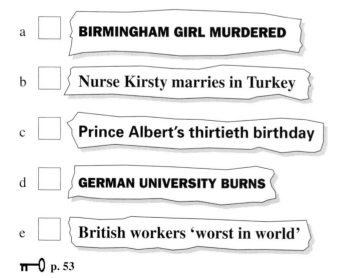

a ⬚ **BIRMINGHAM GIRL MURDERED**

b ⬚ **Nurse Kirsty marries in Turkey**

c ⬚ **Prince Albert's thirtieth birthday**

d ⬚ **GERMAN UNIVERSITY BURNS**

e ⬚ **British workers 'worst in world'**

π⊸ **p. 53**

Listen again and practise saying the headlines.

● **Connected speech**

3 Saying dates

1 Look at the words below. Check the meaning of new words in your dictionary or with your teacher.

saint	lovers	destroy
parliament	war	joke
witch	official	celebrate

2 ⬚ **T.8.3.A.** Below are the names of some special days in Britain. You will hear when they are, and what they celebrate. Listen and write in when they are.

a St Valentine's Day
14 February

e Halloween

b **April Fool's Day**

f **Guy Fawkes Night**

c **St George's Day**

g **Remembrance Sunday**

d The Queen's Birthday

h **St Andrew's Day**

π⊸ **p. 53**

Which ones do you celebrate in your country too?

3 We *write* dates like this.

14 February   1 April

We *say* dates like this.

/ðə/   /əv/
the fourteenth of February

/ðə/   /əv/
the first of April

We use the **weak** forms of *the* and *of* when we say dates. Notice the linking when we speak fast. (See Unit 3.)

/fɔːtiːnθəv/
the fourteenth of February

/fɜːstəveɪprəl/
the first of April

| T.8.3.B. | Listen to the dates above again. Practise saying them, with the weak forms and linking.

π—0 p. 54

4 Write down five dates that are important in your country. Practise saying them correctly. Why are they important?

● Stress and connected speech

4 Reading aloud

1 Can you remember the story of the French burglar from page 56–7 of the Student's Book? Below are all the important words from the story, but the other words are missing.

| T.8.4. | Listen and write in the missing words. If possible, use a pencil.

_____ _____ first _____ June _____

_____ -two, _____ French burglar broke _____

_____ house _____ Paris.

_____ went _____ _____ living _____ _____ stole two pictures. Then _____ went _____ _____ kitchen. _____ opened _____ fridge _____ saw _____ cheese. _____ _____ hungry, _____ _____ ate _____ cheese. Next, _____ saw two bottles _____ champagne. _____ _____ very thirsty, _____ _____ drank both bottles. Then _____ felt sleepy. _____ went upstairs _____ _____ rest, _____ _____ _____ tired _____ fell asleep. When _____ woke up _____ next morning, _____ _____ four policemen around _____ bed.

π—0 p. 54

2 The important words in the story are stressed.

　□　　□　　　　　■
On the first of June nineteen ninety-two,

　□　■　□　　□　■
a French burglar broke into a house in Paris.

　□　■　　□　□■
He went into the living room and stole two pictures.

Listen again to the story, phrase by phrase, and practise reading it, stressing the important words.

3 The words you wrote in the gaps are more difficult to hear because many of them are weak. Many have an /ə/ vowel sound.

　/ə/ /ə/
On the first of June nineteen ninety-two,

/ə/   /ə/   /ə/
a French burglar broke into a house in Paris.

　/ə//ə/   /ə/   /ə/
He went into the living room and stole two pictures.

Listen again, and practise saying the story phrase by phrase. Stress the important words and use the weak forms.

4 Look at your completed story in 1. Read the whole story aloud.

25

UNIT 9

● Sounds

1 Problem vowel sounds: / æ / and / ʌ /

All Nationalities

1 **T.9.1.A.** Listen to the vowel sounds in the words below. Can you hear the difference?

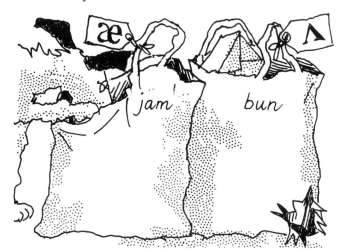

2 **T.9.1.B.** Listen to the food words below. Write them on the correct bag above.

jam	h<u>o</u>ney	c<u>a</u>bbage	b<u>u</u>tter
bun	<u>a</u>pple	carrot	s<u>a</u>lad
<u>o</u>nion	m<u>u</u>shroom	ham	cuc<u>u</u>mber

3 **T.9.1.C.** Listen and check your answers.

🎧 p. 54

4 Complete the rule.

> a The sound / æ / is spelt with the letter ___.
>
> b The sound / ʌ / is usually spelt with the letter ___ but sometimes with the letter ___.

🎧 p. 54

26

5 To make the sound / æ / your lips look like this.

/ æ /

Listen again to the first part. Practise saying the words from bag 1 above.

6 To make the sound / ʌ / your lips look like this.

/ ʌ /

Now listen to the second part. Practise saying the words from bag 2 above.

7 **T.9.1.D.** Listen to the dialogue below. Check the meaning of new words in your dictionary or with your teacher.

Daughter Mum ... what have we got for supper?

Mum Sorry, there's not much ... ham ... scrambled eggs ... or there's some mushroom salad left.

Daughter I'll just have bread and jam ... have we got any butter?

Mum Sorry, love. There's none left.

Daughter Oh Mum! There's nothing I want!

Mum Well, have a nice cup of hot chocolate.

Daughter Mm … **you** make lovely hot chocolate … Thanks Mum!

8   Work with a partner. Find all the words in the dialogue that have an / æ / or an / ʌ / sound. Listen again and check your answers.

🗝 p. 54

9   Practise saying the dialogue line by line, pronouncing the two sounds correctly. Practise reading the dialogue aloud with your partner.

● Connected speech

2 Weak form of *of*

1   Find a word in the box to complete the phrases below.

aspirin	sugar	matches	cake
cigarettes	tea	water	

a piece of _Cake_

a packet of _____

a cup of _____

a glass of _____

a box of _____

a bottle of _____

a bag of _____

🗝 p. 54

2   Look at the stress in these phrases.

☐ ■   ☐ ■
a piece of cake   a packet of cigarettes

T.9.2.A. Listen. *a* and *of* are weak. *of* links with the word before when we speak fast.

/ə/   /əv/   /ə/   /əv/
a piece of cake   a packet of cigarettes

Practise saying the phrases in 1, paying attention to the stress, weak forms, and linking.

3   **T.9.2.B.** Listen and count the words you hear. (*I'd* = two words).

a **7** _____ like

_____ wine?

b ☐ Can _____

_____ coffee, please?

c ☐ _____

bottle _____ aspirin, _____ .

d ☐ _____ packet _____

_____box

_____ , please.

e ☐ Daddy, _____

_____ glass _____?

f ☐ _____

potatoes, please.

g ☐ _____ like

_____?

🗝 p. 54

4 Listen again and write in the missing words.

🗝 p. 54

Practise saying the sentences, paying attention to the stress, weak forms, and linking.

5 Work with a partner. Invent a short dialogue to include each of the sentences above.

Example

Would you like a glass of wine?

Oh, yes please.

Red or white?

A

B

White, please.

28

● **Stress and intonation**

3 Special stress

1 ⬚ T.9.3.A. ⬚ Walter is a waiter in a busy snack bar. Listen to some of his conversations with the customers.

a **W** So that's two coffees, a beef sandwich, and a tomato soup …

C *No, a chicken sandwich.*

W Sorry, sir …

b **W** Yes, sir?

C A small mushroom pizza, please.

W Okay …

C *No, make that a large mushroom pizza.*

W Certainly, sir …

c **W** Okay, so you want one coffee, six colas, four strawberry ice-creams, two chocolate ice-creams and a piece of apple pie …

C *No, four chocolate ice-creams and two strawberry …*

W Anything else?

2 Listen again and look at the lines *in italics*. Underline the words that are specially stressed. Why are these words stressed?

🗝 p. 54

3 **T.9.3.B.** We often use stress and intonation to correct. The intonation goes up and comes down strongly on the word that we want to correct.

No, a <u>chicken</u> sandwich

Make that a <u>large</u> mushroom pizza

No, four <u>choc</u>olate ice-creams and two <u>straw</u>berry …

Practise the stress and intonation in these lines.

4 Work with a partner. Practise the four dialogues, putting in the 'special' stress.

5 You and your partner are a waiter and a customer. The waiter makes a lot of mistakes, so the customer corrects him. Use the food on the cards below.

WAITER	CUSTOMER
a beef sandwich	**a tuna sandwich**
tomato soup	**chicken soup**
three side salads	**two side salads**
a large cheeseburger	**a small baconburger**
two cups of tea and one cup of coffee	**two cups of coffee and one cup of tea**

Example

So you want a beef sandwich?

A

B

No, I want a tuna sandwich!

Remember to stress the words that you want to correct.

4 Polite requests

We use *Could* to make polite requests.

Could you pass the salt?
Could I use the phone?

But in English, intonation is also very important if you want to sound polite.

1 **T.9.4.A.** Listen. All the students in the class want to ask the teacher something – but three of them don't sound polite. Cross (✗) the ones that don't sound polite. Why don't they sound polite?

a Could you lend me a pen, please?

b Could you say that again, please?

c Could you write it on the board, please?

d Could I open the window, please?

e Could you help me with this, please?

f Could you come here, please?

🔑 p. 54

2 To sound polite, intonation must not be flat.

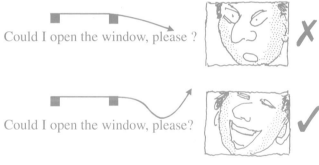

Could I open the window, please? ✗

Could I open the window, please? ✓

Start higher up. Practise by humming, like this.

mm mm mm-mm mm MM-mm mm

Could I open the window, please?

T.9.4.B. Listen and practise the requests with polite intonation.

3 Choose four of the requests above that you think will be useful in your English lesson. You have three minutes to remember them. Practise the polite intonation.

4 Now make the requests to your teacher. He/She will only respond if you sound polite!

29

UNIT 10

● Sounds

1 Problem consonants: / h /

(E) (F) (Gr) (I) (J) (P)

1 **T.10.1.A.** Listen to the pairs of words below. Can you hear the difference?

a	I	(high)		d	ate	hate
b	eat	heat		e	ill	hill
c	air	hair		f	earring	hearing

2 **T.10.1.B.** Listen to the sentences and circle the word you hear.

π—○ p. 54

3 To make the sound / h / you push a lot of air out of your mouth without moving your tongue.

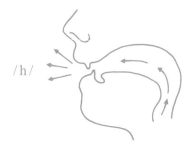

/ h /

◀ **T.10.1.A.** Listen again and practise saying the pairs of words.

4 Read the dialogue below. Check the meaning of new words in your dictionary or with your teacher.

M Who's that with Henry Higgins?

W It's his wife, Hazel.

M Hazel? But his wife's name's Helen!

W Oh no, Helen left him … he's married to Hazel now.

M No! How did it happen?

W Well, you know last Easter, Henry and Helen had a holiday in Honolulu.

M Yes … what happened?

W They had a horrible holiday, and when they arrived home, Helen left him!

M I see … and who are those horrid little girls?

W Holly and Hannah, Hazel's children from her first marriage.

M But Henry *hates* children!

W Mm … how interesting!

5 **T.10.1.C.** Listen and answer these questions.

a Who was Henry's first wife?

b Who is Henry's second wife?

c Are Hannah and Holly …
   … Helen's children?
   … Hazel's children?
   … Henry's children ?

d Does Henry like children?

⚟ p. 54

6 Practise saying the dialogue line by line, pronouncing / h / correctly. Then practise the dialogue with a partner.

● **Word focus**

2 Stress in compound nouns

Many words in English are made by putting two words together. This is called a compound noun.

post + office = post office

1 Take a word from **A** and a word from **B** and put them together to match a picture in column **C**.

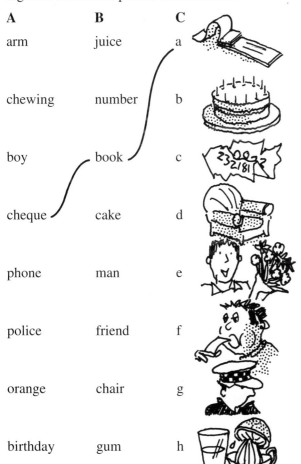

A	B	C
arm	juice	a
chewing	number	b
boy	book	c
cheque	cake	d
phone	man	e
police	friend	f
orange	chair	g
birthday	gum	h

T.10.2. Listen and check your answers.

⚟ p. 54

2 Listen again to the word stress. Is it on the **first** or **second** word?

Circle the correct answer to complete the rule.

> Compound nouns made of noun + noun have the stress on the *first/second* word.

⚟ p. 54

Practise saying the compound nouns paying attention to the stress.

3 Look at the compound nouns below. They are all from the Student's Book. Practise saying them, putting the stress on the **first** word.

	policeman
postcard	**word processor**
	video recorder
credit card	**dining room**
	concert hall
dishwasher	clothes shop
	handbag
schoolteacher	**phone card**
	hairdresser
suitcase	**washing machine**
	birthday card
living room	**book shop**
	nightclub
wine bar	**shop assistant**
	bathroom
post office	**bedroom**
	newsagent's
businessman	**briefcase**

4   Work in groups. Use the words in 3 above. Find:

a 3 places to go in the evening

1. _____	2. _____
3. _____	

b 3 types of bag

1. _____	2. _____
3. _____	

c 4 types of card

1. _____	2. _____
3. _____	4. _____

d 4 machines

1. _____	2. _____
3. _____	4. _____

e 4 rooms

1. _____	2. _____
3. _____	4. _____

f 4 shops

1. _____	2. _____
3. _____	4. _____

g 5 jobs

1. _____	2. _____
3. _____	4. _____
5. _____	

The first group to finish shouts *Stop!* The winning group reads out their answers. If they stress the wrong word in the compound noun, the other groups can shout *Challenge!*

FINISH   FINISH   FINISH   FINISH   FINISH

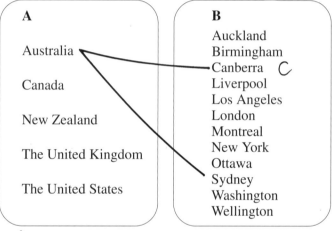 p. 54

● Connected speech

3 Comparatives and superlatives

English-speaking countries

1   Look at the countries in **A** and the cities in **B**.

a Which country are the cities in?

b Which is the capital of each country?

A	**B**
Australia	Auckland
	Birmingham
	Canberra C
Canada	Liverpool
	Los Angeles
New Zealand	London
	Montreal
	New York
The United Kingdom	Ottawa
	Sydney
	Washington
The United States	Wellington

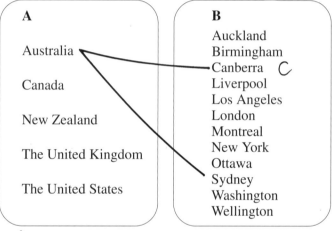 p. 55

2   Look at the questions below. Do you know the answers?

a In area, which is the largest country – Australia, Canada or the USA?

b Which is the smallest country in area – New Zealand or the UK?

c Which country has the smallest population?

d London is the biggest city in the UK. Which is the second biggest – Birmingham or Liverpool?

e Which is the oldest city – New York, Washington or Los Angeles?

f Which has the largest population – London or Los Angeles?

g Which has the largest population – New York or New Zealand?

T.10.3.A.   Listen and find the answers to the questions.

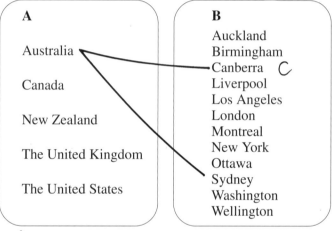 p. 55

3 **T.10.3.B.** Listen to the pronunciation of the comparative and superlative forms of adjectives.

bigger   biggest
higher   highest
larger   largest
older   oldest
smaller   smallest

Look at the comparative and superlative forms in sentences.

◻ ◻/ə/ /ə/ ■
New York is bigger than Washington.

◻ /ə/ /ɪ/ ◻ ◻ ■
New York is the biggest city in the United States.

than and *the* are weak. They have the vowel sound /ə/.

◀ **T.10.3.A.** Look at the tapescript on page 55 and listen to the sentences again. Practise saying them, pronouncing the comparatives and superlatives correctly.

4 Look at the chart below. Make more sentences about these countries.

Examples

Wellington is the smallest city.

In population, the UK is bigger than Australia.

Country	Area	Population	Cities	
Australia	7.7 m. sq.km.	17 m.	Canberra	(303,000)
			Sydney	(3.2 m.)
Canada	9.9 m. sq.km.	25 m.	Ottawa	(819,000)
			Montreal	(980,000)
New Zealand	269,000 sq.km.	3 m.	Wellington	(325,000)
			Auckland	(144,000)
United Kingdom	244,000 sq.km.	56 m.	London	(6.4 m.)
			Birmingham	(920,000)
			Liverpool	(510,000)
United States	9.4 m. sq.km.	249 m.	Washington	(607,000)
			New York	(7 m.)
			Los Angeles	(2.9 m.)

m. = million   sq.km. = square kilometres

(From statistics published in 1991)

5 Answer the questions below about **your** country/city. Use full sentences, and pronounce the comparatives and superlatives correctly.

a Is your city bigger or smaller than Auckland?
b Is it bigger or smaller than Liverpool?
c In population, is your country larger or smaller than the UK?
d Is it larger or smaller than Australia, in population?
e In area, is your country larger or smaller than the UK?
f Which is the biggest city in your country?
g Which is the longest river?
h Which is the highest mountain?
i Which is the nicest part, do you think?

UNIT 11

● Sounds

1 Introduction to diphthongs

T.11.1.A. A diphthong is two vowel sounds put together.

Example /e/ + /ɪ/ = /eɪ/

The first vowel sound is longer than the second. There are eight diphthongs in English.

1 Here are the eight diphthong sounds. Look at the phonemic symbols. Can you guess what the sound is? What is the word in phonemic script?

☐	/eɪ/	/deɪ/ *day*
☐	/aɪ/	/naɪn/ _____
☐	/ɔɪ/	/bɔɪ/ _____
☐	/aʊ/	/naʊ/ _____
☐	/əʊ/	/nəʊ/ _____
☐	/eə/	/heə/ _____
☐	/ɪə/	/hɪə/ _____
☐	/ʊə/*	/tʊə/ _____

T.11.1.B. Listen and tick (✓) the sounds you guessed correctly. Write in the other words.

π—◯ p. 55

* Many native speakers do not use this diphthong. They use /ɔ:/ instead.

2 Cover the words. Can you remember the words for the sounds? Work with a partner. Test your partner by pointing to the symbols.

3 Read the phonemic symbols and match the phrase to the picture.

a ə rɪəl bɪəd <u>7</u>   e ə kəʊld nəʊz ___

b ə leɪzɪ deɪ ___   f ə braɪt laɪt ___

c feə heə ___   g ə laʊd ʃaʊt ___

d nɔɪzɪ bɔɪz ___

1.    5.

2.    6.

3.    7.

4.

T.11.1.C. Listen and check your answers.

π—◯ p. 55

Practise saying the phrases.

4 Look at the phonemic symbols on page 50. Find the words from the box for symbols 37–44. Write them in the spaces under the symbols.

34

2 Problem consonants: / n / and / ŋ /

All Nationalities

1   Look at the pairs of words in the square below. Do you understand the meaning from the pictures? Check the meaning of new words in your dictionary or with your teacher.

T.11.2.A.   Listen. Can you hear the difference?

2   Practise the two sounds. To make / n / and / ŋ /, the air comes out through your nose. Your tongue is further back in your mouth when you make / ŋ /.

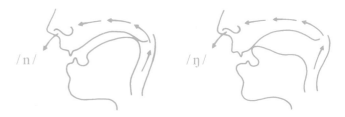

/ n /   / ŋ /

Listen again and practise saying the pairs of words.

1 fans   STAGE DC

2 fangs

3 ran   MARATHON

4 rang   HE SAID HE FINISHED THE RUN

5 son

6 sung   BRAVO

7 ban   DISCO

8 bang   DISCO   BANG

9 Ron   RON

10 wrong

11 win

12 wing

13 thin

14 thing

15 ton   TON

16 tongue

3   **T.11.2.B.**   Listen and circle. Are the sentences true or false?

a (true) false   c true   false   e true   false

b true   false   d true   false   f true   false

π⎯○ **p. 55**

35

2 Problem consonants: / n / and / ŋ /

All Nationalities

1   Look at the pairs of words in the square below. Do you understand the meaning from the pictures? Check the meaning of new words in your dictionary or with your teacher.

T.11.2.A.   Listen. Can you hear the difference?

2   Practise the two sounds. To make / n / and / ŋ /, the air comes out through your nose. Your tongue is further back in your mouth when you make / ŋ /.

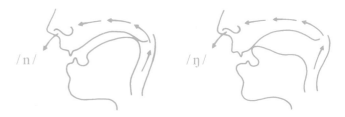

/ n /   / ŋ /

Listen again and practise saying the pairs of words.

3   **T.11.2.B.**   Listen and circle. Are the sentences true or false?

a (true) false   c true   false   e true   false

b true   false   d true   false   f true   false

π⎯○ **p. 55**

4 Work in pairs. Make some statements about the pictures yourself. Your partner will say if they are true or false.

5 Look at the phonemic symbols on page 50. Find the word from the box for sound 24. Write it in the space under the symbol.

● **Connected speech**

3 Short forms (contractions)

1 Look at the sentences below. They are all wrong – why?

a I got two children.

b I have a coffee, please.

c She nineteen years old.

d I very hungry.

e I like two cokes, please.

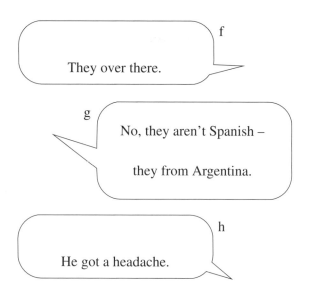

f They over there.

g No, they aren't Spanish – they from Argentina.

h He got a headache.

Write in the missing short forms, like this.

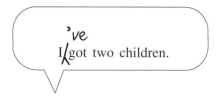

've
I̸got two children.

T.11.3.A. Listen and check your answers.
π─◯ p. 55

2 **T.11.3.B.** You will hear some foreign students saying the sentences. Three of them are wrong because the contraction is not pronounced. Listen and tick (✔) the box if the contraction is pronounced, and cross (✘) the box if it is not pronounced.

a ☐   d ☐   g ☐
b ☐   e ☐   h ☐
c ☐   f ☐

π─◯ p. 55

3 ◀ **T.11.3.A.** Listen to the correct forms again and practise saying them. Pay attention to the pronunciation of the short forms.

UNIT 12

● Sounds

1 Problem vowel and diphthong sounds: / ɒ /, / ɔː /, and / əʊ /

All Nationalities

1 **T.12.1.A.** Listen to the three sounds. Can you hear the difference?

/ dʒɒn /	/ dʒɔːdʒ /	/ dʒəʊ /
John	George	Jo

Practise saying the three names.

2 **T.12.1.B.** Listen and answer the questions about John, George, and Jo. (The sounds / ɒ /, / ɔː /, and / əʊ / will help you!)

Who …

… is from **Do**ver?	John	George	<u>Jo</u>
… is from **Bo**ston?	John	George	Jo
… was b**or**n in Y**or**k?	John	George	Jo
… drinks w**a**ter?	John	George	Jo
… drinks **Co**ca-**Co**la?	John	George	Jo
… drinks **co**ffee?	John	George	Jo
… plays p**o**lo?	John	George	Jo
… likes g**o**lf and h**o**ckey?	John	George	Jo

… likes **a**ll sp**or**ts?	John	George	Jo
… sm**o**kes a lot?	John	George	Jo
… t**a**lks a lot?	John	George	Jo
… eats a lot of **cho**colate?	John	George	Jo

⊓⊙ p. 55

3 Work in pairs. Ask each other questions, like this.

● Sounds and spelling

2 Words ending in the sound / ə /

1 Look at the words in the box. How is the last syllable pronounced in each word?

camera	answer	*picture*
mirror	sister	opera
centre	colour	**flavour**
actor	jumper	hamburger
tuna	signature	departure

T.12.2. Listen and practise saying the words.

2 Put the words into the columns below according to their spelling.

1 -er	2 -or	3 -a

4 -ure	5 -re	6 -our

WORD RACE

3 Work in groups.

Use the word list at the back of the Student's Book to help you. Find:

10 more words to go in Column 1.

3 more words to go in Column 2.

3 more words to go in Column 3.

1 more word to go in Columns 4, 5, and 6.

The first group to finish shouts *Stop!*

FINISH   FINISH   FINISH   FINISH   FINISH

4 Practise saying your words. Pay attention to the /ə/ sound at the end.

● Connected speech

3 Weak form of *to*

1 Match the parts in **A** and **B** below to make full sentences.

A	**B**
a I'm going out	1. to see the manager.
b They're waiting	2. to buy a newspaper.
c My daughter's studying	3. to go out with her boyfriend.
d My brother's going abroad	4. to meet some friends.
e We're going to the airport	5. to work.
f She's getting ready	6. to become a doctor.

T.12.3.A. Listen and check your answers.

 p. 55

2 Listen again. Note the pronunciation of *to* at the beginning of **B**. Is it strong or weak?

 p. 55

Practise saying the sentences pronouncing *to* correctly.

Start with *to* like this.

/ təbaɪ /
to buy ... to buy ... to buy
to buy a newspaper
out to buy a newspaper
I'm going out to buy a newspaper

Practise saying the other sentences in the same way.

3 T.12.3.B. The weak *to* is used in other contexts. Listen to the dialogue below and write in the missing *to*s as in the example. There are six more.

D Where are you going, Dad?

F To the station meet Mum.

D Oh, what time's her train?

F Twenty five. Do you want come?

D No, I've got go the doctor's at quarter five.

F Oh, yes, well, see you later!

D See you!

 p. 55

4 Listen again and practise the dialogue line by line. Pay attention to the pronunciation of *to*. Read the dialogue aloud with a partner.

● Intonation

4 Sounding enthusiastic

1 | **T.12.4.** | Listen to these conversations at a party. Fill in the gaps in the suggestions below.

1A Let's _____!

1B Okay then!

2A Shall we go into the _____?

2B Okay.

3A Let's have another _____!

3B Okay!

4A Come on, Susie, let's ____ _____!

4B Okay, just a minute.

5A Shall we have a _____ soon?

5B Okay, if you want to.

6A Shall we start the _____ ____?

6B Okay, if you want to.

π-O **p. 55**

2 **B** always answers *Okay*, but does **B** really want to do what **A** suggests? Listen again and tick (✓) if **B** really **is** enthusiastic about the suggestion, and cross (✗) the dialogues where **B** isn't really enthusiastic.

1. ✓   3. ☐   5. ☐

2. ☐   4. ☐   6. ☐

π-O **p. 55**

3 In the dialogues where **B** is not enthusiastic, the voice starts low.

Okay

To show enthusiasm, the voice starts high and goes down and then up again, like this.

Okay

Listen again and repeat what **B** says. Copy the intonation. Practise the dialogues with a partner.

4 Your teacher* will make some suggestions to you. You must always answer *Okay*. Use intonation to show if you're really enthusiastic.

5 Make a suggestion yourself. See how the class responds!

* See the Answer key on page 55.

UNIT 13

● Sounds

1 Problem vowel and diphthong sounds: / e / and / eɪ /

Ⓓ Ⓕ Ⓗ Ⓘ

1 **T.13.1.A.** Listen to the pairs of words below. Can you hear the difference?

pen	pain
tell	tail
wet	wait

2 Now look at these words. Check the meaning of new words in your dictionary or with your teacher.

T.13.1.B. Listen and circle the word you hear.

a   men   main

b   let   late

c   get   gate

d   sell   sail

🔑 **p. 55**

3 You make the sound / e / at the front of your mouth. Your lips look like this.

To make the sound / eɪ / first make a long / e / sound and then a short / ɪ / sound.

Now practise saying the pairs of words in 1.

4 **T.13.1.C.** Listen to Jenny talking about her holiday. Are the **bold** sounds / e / or / eɪ /? Mark the / e / sounds like this ⎯ and the / eɪ / sounds like this ⌇⌇.

Last year, I w**e**nt to Sp**ai**n on holid**ay** with my fri**e**nd

J**a**ne. The hotel was gr**ea**t, but the w**ea**ther was

terrible! It r**ai**ned **e**very d**ay** for t**e**n d**ay**s!

🔑 **p. 56**

5 The sentences below are about Unit 13 of the Student's Book, but they are all false. How many examples of / e / and / eɪ / can you find? Mark them in the same way as 4.

a An African elephant weighs ten tonnes.

b Elvis Presley played jazz.

c The train from Newcastle to London takes eight hours.

d Laurel and Hardy met in the USA in 1928.

e Julie read about the weather in Liverpool.

🔑 **p. 56**

6 Look back at Unit 13 of the Student's Book, and make the sentences true.

T.13.1.D. Listen and check your answers.

🔑 **p. 56**

Practise reading the true sentences. Pay attention to the / e / and / eɪ / sounds.

2 Problem consonants: / ʃ / and / tʃ /

Ⓓ Ⓔ Ⓕ Ⓖⓡ Ⓘ

1 **T.13.2.A.** Listen to these words.

> shirt   sugar   delicious
> dishwasher   pronunciation

The sound / ʃ / is often spelt *sh*. What other ways is it spelt?

🔑 p. 56

2 Look at the text about Sheila. How many examples of the / ʃ / sound can you hear? Underline them.

Sheila is a receptionist at the International Hotel in Chicago. At the moment she's studying Spanish.

T.13.2.B. Listen and check your answers.

🔑 p. 56

3 To make the sound / ʃ / first practise / s /. Now move your tongue back and up a little. It is the sound we make when we want people to be quiet!

Practise reading the text aloud, paying attention to the / ʃ / sound.

4 **T.13.2.C.** Listen. Can you hear the difference?

she's   cheese   sheep   cheap

shoes   choose   wash   watch

The second word in each pair has the sound / tʃ /. To make the sound / tʃ /, first say / t /. Then say / ʃ /. Repeat each sound quickly until you say the two sounds together. The sound / tʃ / is usually spelt *ch*.

5 Look at the picture below. Can you find:

a Spanish beach?   Sheila catching a fish?
some Scottish children?   an English teacher?
a Frenchman eating cheese?   a pair of cheap shoes?
two Chinese men playing chess?

T.13.2.D. Listen to the phrases. Underline the sound / ʃ / like this ▁ and the sound / tʃ / like this ∿.

🔑 p. 56

6 Practise saying the words. Work in pairs, like this.

7 Look at the phonemic symbols on page 50. Find the words from the box for sounds 20 and 22. Write them in the spaces under the symbols.

● Sounds and spelling

3 The sound / ə / in final syllables

1 Write in the missing letters.

a American

___German___   ___Mexican___

b seas__n

_____   _____

c childr__n

_____   _____

d music____n

_____   _____

e televis____n

_____   _____

f conversat____n

_____   _____

g beautif__l

_____   _____

h nation__l

_____   _____

i intellig__nt

_____   _____

j nerv____s

_____   _____

π⊙ p. 56

2 The final syllable in the words in 1 is spelt differently in each word, but the vowel sound in the final syllable is always / ə /.

| / ə / | / ə / | / ə / | / ə / |
| American | season | children | musician |

T.13.3.A. Listen and practise saying the words. Pay attention to the sound / ə / in the final syllables.

3 Look at the box below and find **two** words with the same ending as each word above. Write them in the spaces in exercise 1.

German	successful	London	decision
listen	station	optician	revision
arrival	parent	careful	pardon
Mexican	garden	student	famous
delicious	hospital	beautician	pronunciation

T.13.3.B. Listen and check your answers.
π⊙ p. 56

Practise saying the words. Can you think of any more words to put in each group?

4 Think of phrases with these words.

Examples

a successful student
a famous garden
a German hospital

Practise saying the phrases.

● Connected speech

4 Linking (revision)

1 Look at the words below. Check the meaning of new words in your dictionary or with your teacher.

> absolutely   ambulance   attractive
> awful   excellent   experience
> immediately   incredible   area

2 **T.13.4.** You will hear some sentences. If they have an adjective, write *adj*; if they have an adverb, write *adv*; and if they have an adjective and an adverb, write *both*.

a _*adj*_   e _____

b _____   f _____

c _____   g _____

d _____   h _____

π—◯ p. 56

3 Listen again and fill in the gaps in the sentences.

a What a _____ _____!

b It was an _____ _____.

c The weather was _____ _____!

d He got into their _____ _____.

e She speaks _____ _____ and

_____.

f It was an _____ _____!

g She lives in a _____ _____

_____.

h I'll phone for an _____ _____!

π—◯ p. 56

4 Notice the linking between words **A** and **B**.

A	B	A	B
What a		fantastic	idea

What kind of sound does **A** end with? What kind of sound does **B** begin with?

π—◯ p. 56

5 Look at the other sentences in 3 and mark the linking.

π—◯ p. 56

Listen again and practise putting in the linking.

6 Look at the dialogue below from page 98 of the Student's Book. Mark five examples of this kind of linking.

Hello. I'd like a ticket to Newcastle, please.

Single or return?

Return, please.

Day return or period return?

I want to come back this evening, so a day return.

How do you want to pay?

Cash, please.

Forty-eight pounds fifty, please.

Twenty, forty, sixty pounds.

Here's your change and your ticket.

Thank you.

π—◯ p. 56

UNIT 14

● Sounds

1 Problem consonants: /tʃ/, /dʒ/, and /j/

Ⓓ Ⓔ Ⓕ Ⓖⓡ Ⓗ Ⓟ

1 **T.14.1.A.** Listen to the words below. Can you hear the difference between the three consonant sounds?

/tʃ/	/dʒ/	/j/
Chess	Jess	Yes

2 Say the three words. Which ones are most difficult for you? Practise saying these again.

To make /j/ first start with the sound /iː/.

i i i … yes
i i … yes
i … yes

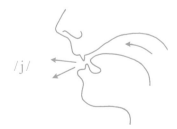

/j/

You practised /dʒ/ in Unit 8.1, and /tʃ/ in 13.2. Remember that you use your voice for /dʒ/ but you do not use your voice for /tʃ/.

3 **T.14.1.B.** The words below are similar in many languages. In English they all begin with one of the sounds above: /tʃ/, /dʒ/ or /j/. Listen and write the correct symbol in the box.

a [tʃ] chocolate

b [ ] yoga

c [ ] chimpanzee

d [ ] yacht

e [ ] jacket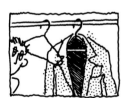

f [ ] chess

g ☐ yoghurt

h ☐ gin

i ☐ geography

j ☐ jeans

⚷ p. 56

4 Complete the rule with the correct phonemic symbols. Add an example from the words in 3.

> **Spelling rule**
>
> a The letter *y* (at the beginning of a word) is pronounced / /.
>
>   **Example** _____
>
> b 1. The letter *j* is pronounced / /.
>
>   **Example** _____
>
>   2. The letters *ge* and *gi* are often pronounced / /.
>
>   **Examples** _____, _____
>
> c The letters *ch* are often pronounced / /.
>
>   **Example** _____
>
> **There are some exceptions, however.**
> *ch* = / k / in *chemist, character, Christmas.*
> *ch* = / ʃ / in *chef, champagne.*
> *ch* = not pronounced in *yacht.*

⚷ p. 56

5 Practise saying the words in 3 above. Remember the rules.

6 Look at the phonemic symbols on page 50. Find the word from the box for sound 17. Write it in the space under the symbol.

---

2 Words with similar vowel sounds

1 The pairs of words below are easy to confuse. Do you remember what they all mean? Tick (✓) the ones you're sure you can pronounce correctly. Put a question mark (**?**) next to the ones you're not sure about.

☐ angry   ☐ hungry

☐ leave   ☐ live

☐ this   ☐ these

☐ where   ☐ were

☐ want   ☐ won't

☐ walk   ☐ work

T.14.2.A. Listen and check. Practise saying the pairs of words.

2 **T.14.2.B.** Now listen and put the words into the correct box below.

1	2	3
4	5	6
7	8	9
10	11	12

⚷ p. 56

3 Play the game with a partner. Your partner must tell you where to write the words.

1	2	3
4	5	6
7	8	9
10	11	12

● Connected speech

3 Contractions and weak forms in the Present Perfect

1 **T.14.3.A.** Listen to the sentences below. You will hear each one twice. One time *have/has/haven't/hasn't* is pronounced correctly. The other time it is pronounced incorrectly. Which is correct? Tick **a** or **b**.

1. I've never seen it.   a ✓   b ☐

2. She's just come back.   a ☐   b ☐

3. He hasn't phoned yet.   a ☐   b ☐

4. We haven't been here.   a ☐   b ☐

5. Has your sister gone out?   a ☐   b ☐

6. Yes, she has.   a ☐   b ☐

7. Have you been to the shops?   a ☐   b ☐

8. Yes, I have.   a ☐   b ☐

⌐O p. 57

Notice the pronunciation of the contractions.

I've = /aɪv/   haven't = /hævənt/
He's = /hi:z/   hasn't = /hæzənt/

In questions, the weak form is used.

/həv/
Have you been to the shops?

/həz/
Has your sister gone out?

In short answers *have* and *has* are strong.

    /hæv/   /hæz/
    ■   ■
Yes, I have.   Yes, she has.

2 **T.14.3.B.** Listen now to the correct sentences only and practise the pronunciation of *have/haven't*, etc.

3 **T.14.3.C.** Listen to a dialogue between two neighbours. They are talking about holidays in Italy. Look at the words below. Underline the things that they talk about.

> pasta   gondolas   the Pope
> the beaches   the Colosseum   Italian clothes
> Pompeii   the Leaning Tower of Pisa

4 Listen again.

a How many times do you hear *have* or *has*?

b How many times do you hear *'ve* or *'s*?

c How many times do you hear *haven't* or *hasn't*?

Put a tick (✓) in the correct box below each time you hear these forms.

have or *has*	
've or *'s*	
haven't or *hasn't*	

⌐O p. 57

5 Work with a partner. Look at the tapescript of the dialogue on page 57 and practise it with a partner. Pay attention to the pronunciation of the different forms of *have*.

UNIT 15

● Word focus

1 Word stress (revision)

1 Can you remember the words below? Look at the stress. Which one is correct in British English? Cross out the incorrectly stressed words.

1. a ~~address~~   b address
2. a afternoon   b afternoon
3. a cassette   b cassette
4. a credit card   b credit card
5. a dessert   b dessert
6. a dictionary   b dictionary
7. a hotel   b hotel
8. a Japan   b Japan
9. a photographer   b photographer
10. a policeman   b policeman
11. a post office   b post office
12. a vegetable   b vegetable

T.15.1.A. Listen and check. How many did you guess correctly?

🎧 p. 57

2 Listen again and write the / ə / sounds in the correct words, like this.

/ə/ ●
address

🎧 p. 57

Practise saying the words.

3 **T.15.1.B.** Listen to some foreign students using the words. Tick (✓) the box if the stress on the word is correct. Cross (✗) the box if it is wrong.

a ☐   Have you got a *dictionary*?

b ☐   Do you want any more *vegetables*?

c ☐   Could I borrow this *cassette*?

d ☐   Do you know the *address* of your hotel?

e ☐   My brother's a *policeman*.

f ☐   I think I left my *credit card* in the post office.

🎧 p. 57

Practise saying the sentences correctly.

47

● Stress and connected speech

2 Reading aloud (revision)

1　T.15.2.A. Look back at the letter from Paula to her parents on page 109 of the Student's Book. Paula's mother is reading it aloud to her father. Listen to the first part.

Look at the text of the first paragraph.

> <u>Dear</u> Mum and <u>Dad</u>,
>
> I'm <u>really</u> <u>sorry</u>, but I'm <u>leaving</u> <u>home</u>. <u>When</u> you
>
> <u>read</u> this, I'll be <u>far</u> <u>away</u>. <u>Don't</u> try to <u>find</u> me.
>
> <u>Martin</u> and I are <u>getting</u> <u>married</u> next <u>Saturday</u>.

The stressed (strong) words are underlined.

☐ ■
<u>Dear</u> Mum and <u>Dad</u>
MM mm　mm　MM

These are the most important words.

2　T.15.2.B. Listen and practise in short sections. First just mumble (MM mm mm MM), but pay attention to the stressed words.

Practise again, reading the words properly.

3　T.15.2.C. Now look at the text of the second paragraph and listen to Paula's mother again. Underline the stressed words as in 1.

> I know you've never liked Martin. You didn't
> want me to go out with him because you said he
> was just a car salesman and he wasn't good
> enough for me. I know that you've always
> wanted the best for me, but Martin is best for me.
> I love him very much indeed.

⚷ p. 57

Listen again and practise in short sections, mumbling the stress.

4　Look at page 109 of the Student's Book and read the rest of the letter in the same way.

● Sounds

3 Phonemic symbols (revision)

1　Before you start the game on the next page you have five minutes to study the phonemic alphabet on page 50. Ask your teacher about anything that you can't remember.

Work in pairs. You have fifteen minutes to do as many activities as you can.

JUST FOR FUN

/ dʒʌst fə fʌn /

1 Which is the odd word out in each circle? Underline it.

a / teɪbl / / tʃeə / / kæt / / kɑːpɪt /

b / tiː / / ɒrɪndʒ dʒuːs / / kɒfɪ / / treɪn /

c / nɜːs / / sekrətrɪ / / flaʊə / / bɪznɪsmən /

d / skuːl / / bred / / ʃɒp / / tʃɜːtʃ /

e / fʊtbɔːl / / tenɪs / / skiːɪŋ / / tɔːkɪŋ /

10 marks: two for each odd word that you found.

2 Match the short forms to the correct phonemic transcription.

don't   / kɑːnt /
           / wɜːrənt /
won't   / dʌznt /
           / dəʊznt /
can't   / wɜːnt /
           / dəʊnt /
weren't   / waʊnt /
doesn't   / kænt /

5 marks: one for each correct transcription that you found.

3 How many times is the sound on the left in each sentence? Underline them.

/ɔː/ a Paul's taller than George.

/ɪ/ b Did you finish your fish and chips?

/ð/ c There's another thing.

/ʌ/ d Your son's just rung up.

/ɜː/ e What's the first word you heard?

/dʒ/ f John's got yoghurt on his jacket and jeans.

10 marks: half for each sound that you found.

4 Find the couples. They have the same vowel sound in their names! Draw a line to match them.

Bill   Dave   Frank   Steve   Eddie

Ann   Jean   Wendy   Lynn   Jane

5 marks: one for each couple that you found.

5 Read the secret message.

ðɪs ɪz ə siːkrɪt mesɪdʒ

ɪf juː nəʊ ɔːl ðə fəniːmɪk sɪmbəlz juː dəʊnt niːd tə stʌdɪ peɪdʒ fɪftɪ əgen.

10 marks if you understood the message.

p. 57

● Phonemic symbols

Consonants

1 / p /	2 / b /	3 / t /	4 / d /	5 / k /	6 / g /	7 / f /	8 / v /
9 / s /	10 / z /	11 / l /	12 / m /	13 / n /	14 / h /	15 / r /	16 / w /
17 / j /	18 / θ /	19 / ð /	20 / ʃ /	21 / ʒ /	22 / tʃ /	23 / dʒ /	24 / ŋ /
				television			

Vowels

25 / i: /	26 / ɪ /	27 / e /	28 / æ /	29 / ɑ: /	30 / ɒ /	31 / ɔ: /	32 / ʊ /
33 / u: /	34 / ʌ /	35 / ɜ: /	36 / ə /				

Diphthongs

37 / eɪ /	38 / əʊ /	39 / aɪ /	40 / aʊ /	41 / ɔɪ /	42 / ɪə /	43 / eə /	44 / ʊə /

Look at the sound underlined in the words below.
Put the words under the correct symbol for that sound.

<u>m</u>an	wh<u>y</u>	<u>th</u>at	<u>t</u>icket	<u>st</u>art	<u>ch</u>oose	<u>j</u>eans	<u>s</u>ing	<u>t</u>our	tele<u>v</u>ision
<u>tea</u>	pen<u>c</u>il	<u>b</u>ag	<u>sh</u>oe	<u>i</u>s	<u>l</u>ike	<u>r</u>ead	<u>w</u>e	<u>y</u>ellow	<u>h</u>air
g<u>oo</u>d	live<u>s</u>	b<u>e</u>d	<u>f</u>ive	d<u>o</u>	<u>s</u>it	<u>th</u>ree	<u>d</u>oor	si<u>s</u>ter	<u>v</u>ocabulary
ha<u>n</u>d	<u>g</u>o	<u>k</u>ey	n<u>o</u>t	<u>y</u>our	lo<u>v</u>e	<u>Gr</u>eece	<u>g</u>irl	da<u>y</u>	<u>n</u>o
<u>d</u>own	<u>h</u>ot	n<u>oi</u>se	b<u>ee</u>r						

KEY

UNIT 1

2

1 1. b 2. a 3. a 4. c
   5. a 6. a 7. b 8. c

3 ● photograph ● passport ● cigarette
   ● toilet ● radio

3

2 b finishes first.
   c finishes second.
   a finishes third.

   T.1.3.B.

   fifty … fifty
   thirteen … thirteen
   seventeen … seventeen
   thirty … thirty
   eighteen … eighteen
   fifteen … fifteen
   ninety … ninety
   sixteen … sixteen
   fourteen … fourteen
   nineteen … nineteen
   eighty … eighty
   sixty … sixty
   forty … forty
   seventy … seventy

4

2 **T.1.4.B.**

   Hello. I'm Jane. This is my cat.
   Her name's Pepper. She's three
   years old and she's very
   intelligent, I think!
   That's my dog, Sam. Sam's twelve
   years old now! He's a very nice
   dog, but he's very stupid.

UNIT 2

2

2 hairdresser nurse
   engineer doctor
   journalist director
   artist interpreter
   receptionist writer

3 Words where *r* **is** pronounced:
   Drive from different countries
   France Briscall very address
   Browns children Catherine
   Andrew friendly interesting
   Green Underground horrible
   Write

   Words where *r* is **not** pronounced:
   October Dear are international
   other They're Argentina
   Switzerland teacher Peter
   letter fourteen Underground
   understand weather parks centre

3

2 ● /ə/
   hamburger

   ● /ə/
   pizza

   ●/ə/
   salads

   ● /ə/ ●/ə/
   mineral water

   ●/ə/ ●/ə/
   Coca-Cola

3 a 3 b 8 c 4 d 9 e 7
   f 2 g 10 h 1 i 5 j 6

4 a, b, c, e, g, and h have an /ə/
   sound.

5 ● potato ● orange
   ● pepper ● banana
   ● yoghurt ● chocolate
   ● chicken ● coffee
   ● tuna ● sandwich

4

3 ☐ ■
   Where are you from?

   ☐ ■
   What's your job?

   ■ ☐
   How old are you?

   ☐ ■
   Are you married?

UNIT 3

1

1 a cups /s/
     pens /z/
     stamps /s/

   b speaks /s/
     reads /z/
     likes /s/

   c Anna's /z/ friend
     Jane's /z/ bag
     Pete's /s/ Mum

   d It's /s/ here.
     How's /z/ Andy?
     He's /z/ okay.

3

1 get up – go to bed
   open – close
   arrive – leave
   start – finish

2 a 6 b 7 c 7 d 7
   e 6 f 7 g 7 h 7

3 **T.3.3.A.**

   a The bank opens at nine o'clock.
   b He goes to bed at seven o'clock.
   c This office closes at half past
      two.
   d We get up at about eight o'clock.
   e Her plane arrives at two fifteen.
   f The programme finishes at
      about elcvcn thirty.
   g The film starts at half past eight.
   h My train leaves at about eleven
      o'clock.

6 e Her plane arrives at two fifteen.

   f The programme finishes at
      about eleven thirty.

   g The film starts at half past eight.

   h My train leaves at about eleven
      o'clock.

4

1 a statement – question
   b statement   question
   c question – statement
   d question – statement

UNIT 4

1

1 a /iː/ and /uː/ are long sounds.

2 a /iː/   e /ʊ/
   b /e/   f /uː/
   c /ɪ/   g /iː/
   d /ɪ/ /ə/   h /ʊ/

2

1 T.4.2.A.

   a **A** Do you know the time?
      B It's quarter past three.

   b **A** Do you have a light?
      B No, sorry.

   c **A** Do you speak English?
      B Yes, a little.

   d **A** Do you understand?
      B Not really.

   e **A** Do you have milk?
      B Yes, please.

   f **A** What do you do?
      B I'm a musician.

3

1 T.4.3.A.

   M Do you have children, Shirley?
   S Yes, a son and a daughter.
   M Oh, that's nice, what do they do?
   S My daughter Jenny's a music teacher, and Michael, my son, is at college – he wants to be a pilot!
   M Oh, lovely!
   S Yes ...
   M Do they live at home?
   S Michael lives with me, but Jenny lives in London – she's married with two children.
   M Oh! So you're a grandmother!
   S Yes, she has a girl and a boy too – Rebecca and Thomas.
   M Oh, lovely – how old are they?
   S The girl's seven and the boy's two – do you want to see a photo?
   M Oh yes. ... Ah ... aren't they beautiful!

4

1

2 interesting 3   camera 2
   restaurant 2   Wednesday 2
   February 3   every 2
   dictionary 3   soldier 2
   chocolate 2   married 2
   vegetables 3

3 ● in**te**resting   ● **cam**era
   ● **res**taurant   ● **Wed**nesday
   ● **Feb**ruary   ● **e**very
   ● **dic**tionary   ● **sol**dier
   ● **choc**olate   ● **mar**ried
   ● **veg**etables

4 a 1 /ɑːnt/
   b 2 /iːvnɪŋ/
   c 2 /feɪvrɪt/
   d 3 /kʌmftəbl/
   e 2 /fæmlɪ/
   f 3 /sekrətrɪ/

UNIT 5

1

2 word – curtain
   four – wall
   man – lamp
   bus – cup
   part – carpet
   shop – pots

4 T.5.1.C.
   1. bath   7. mirror
   2. garden   8. fridge
   3. living room   9. cooker
   4. door   10. washing
   5. cupboard   machine
   6. television

3

3 T.5.3.B.

Desk 1
Hello. Can I help you?
Yes, please. Is the Museum of Modern Art near here?
Mmm, just a minute ... here's a map ...

Desk 2
Next, please.
Hello, can you help me? I want a hotel for three nights.
Sorry, we don't have information about hotels. Try next door.
Thank you.

Desk 3
Excuse me ...
Yes, sir?
Is there a bookshop near here?
Sure, on the left opposite the underground station.

UNIT 6

1

1 a <u>W</u>endy <u>w</u>as <u>tw</u>enty-<u>o</u>ne <u>W</u>ednesday

   b <u>Wh</u>ere <u>w</u>as <u>W</u>illiam <u>w</u>eekend

   c <u>W</u>e <u>w</u>ant <u>W</u>ayne <u>W</u>e <u>w</u>ant <u>W</u>ayne

   d <u>Wh</u>at <u>w</u>onderful <u>w</u>orld

2

1 when i   swim j
   week h   whole k
   wrong e   two b
   who c   what l
   winter d   twenty g
   we a   write f

2 Words with a silent *w*:
wrong   who   whole   two   write

3 a wrong   b whole

4 ┌─────────┐
  │ T.6.2. │
  └─────────┘
(You hear the words in 2 above.)

3

1 a ✓   b ✓   c ✓   d ✗   e ✗
  f ✗   g ✓   h ✓   i ✓   j ✗
  k ✓   l ✓   m ✗

2 a were   h could
  b were   i could
  c were   j couldn't
  d weren't   k can
  e wasn't   l can
  f couldn't   m can't
  g was

UNIT 7

1

2 a sit   c bean   e heel
  b hit   d ship   f lick

4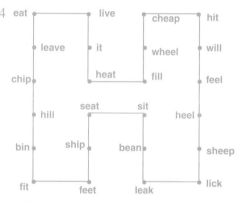

┌─────────┐
│ T.7.1.B. │
└─────────┘

Start at *eat* … draw a line from *eat*
to *live* … then from *live* to *it* … from
it draw a line to *heat* … and from
heat to *fill* … then go from *fill* to
wheel … and from *wheel* to *cheap* …
from *cheap* draw a line to *hit* … then
from *hit* go to *will* … and from *will*
to *feel* … then to *heel* … then to
sheep … and down to *lick* … okay?
Right, now go to *leak* … then from
leak to *bean* … and from *bean* to *sit*
… from *sit* go to *seat* … and then
from *seat* go to *ship* and down to
feet … all right? Now from *feet* you
go to *fit* … from *fit* you go up to *bin*
… then *hill* … then up to *chip* … then
to *leave* … and then finally back up
to *eat* … what have you got?

2

1 a read   f heard
  b learnt   g bought
  c ran   h said
  d fell   i taught
  e saw   j thought

3 ┌───────────┐
  │ T.7.2.A. │
  └───────────┘
(You hear a–f as in 1 above.)

4 ┌───────────┐
  │ T.7.2.B. │
  └───────────┘
(You hear g–j as in 1 above.)

3

2 /t/   /d/

4 ┌──────────┐
  │ T.7.3.C. │
  └──────────┘
  a arrived   d closed
  b opened   e start
  c finish   f stopped

4

2 1. c   2. b   3. c   4. a
  5. a   6. c   7. a

┌──────────┐
│ T.7.4.B. │
└──────────┘

1. Where were you born?
   In New York.

2. When was your sister born?
   In 1978.

3. When was your birthday?
   In March.

4. When did her grandfather die?
   Last year.

5. How old was he?
   About 80.

6. Where did you go to university?
   In London.

7. When did you leave university?
   In 1993.

UNIT 8

1

2 a John Lennon
  b Mick Jagger
  c Jack Kennedy
  d Janet Jackson
  e Julia Roberts
  f Jane Fonda

2

1 No. In British English the *r* is not
  pronounced. In American English
  it **is** pronounced.

2 Thursday   birthday
  person   journey
  university   hamburger
  Germany   thirtieth
  journalist

  There is no /ɜ/ sound in *Saturday*,
  restaurant, and *conversation*.

4 a 3: Birmingham   girl   murdered
  b 3: Nurse   Kirsty   Turkey
  c 2: thirtieth   birthday
  d 3: German   university   burns
  e 3: workers   worst   world

3

2 ┌──────────┐
  │ T.8.3.A. │
  └──────────┘

a St Valentine's Day is the day of
  lovers – it's on the fourteenth of
  February.

b April Fool's Day, on the first of
  April, is a day when people play
  jokes on their friends and families.

c St George's Day is on the twenty-
  third of April – St George is the
  patron saint of England.

d The Queen has an official
  birthday on the second of June but
  her real birthday is on the twenty-
  first of April.

e Halloween is on the thirty-first
  of October – it's a night when
  witches are supposed to come out!

f On Guy Fawkes Night we
  remember the time when a man
  called Guy Fawkes tried to
  destroy the Houses of Parliament.
  It's on the fifth of November.

g Remembrance Sunday is the day
  when we remember all the
  people who died in the First and
  Second World Wars. It's always
  on the second Sunday in
  November.

h St Andrew's Day is on the
  thirtieth of November –
  St Andrew is the patron saint of
  Scotland ... and Russia!

3 T.8.3.B.

/əʊ/
the fourteenth of February

/əʊ/
the first of April

/əʊ/
the twenty-third of April

/əʊ/
the second of June

/əʊ/
the twenty-first of April

/əʊ/
the thirty-first of October

/əʊ/
the fifth of November

/əʊ/
the thirtieth of November

4

1 T.8.4.

On the first of June nineteen ninety-two, a French burglar broke into a house in Paris.

He went into the living room and stole two pictures. Then he went into the kitchen. He opened the fridge and saw some cheese. He was hungry, so he ate the cheese. Next, he saw two bottles of champagne. He was very thirsty, so he drank both bottles. Then he felt sleepy. He went upstairs for a rest, but he was tired and fell asleep. When he woke up the next morning, there were four policemen around the bed.

UNIT 9

1

3 T.9.1.C.

Bag 1	Bag 2
jam	bun
apple	onion
cabbage	honey
carrot	mushroom
ham	butter
salad	cucumber

4 a *a*   b *u*   *o*

8 /æ/
ham scrambled salad have jam thanks

/ʌ/
Mum supper much mushroom just butter love none nothing cup lovely

2

1 a piece of cake
a packet of cigarettes
a cup of tea
a glass of water
a box of matches
a bottle of aspirin
a bag of sugar

3 a 7   b 8   c 8   d 10
e 8   f 5   g 7

4 T.9.2.B.

a Would you like a glass of wine?
b Can I have a cup of coffee, please?
c I'd like a bottle of aspirin, please.
d A packet of cigarettes and a box of matches, please.
e Daddy, can I have a glass of milk?
f A bag of potatoes, please.
g Would you like a piece of cake?

3

2 a chicken
b large
c chocolate strawberry

These words are stressed because the speaker wants to correct a mistake.

4

1 Students c, d, and f do not sound polite.

UNIT 10

1

2 a high   d hate
b eat   e hill
c air   f earring

T.10.1.B.

a It's high!
b Can you eat this?
c This air's very dirty.
d I hate it.
e Did you say *hill*?
f She's got a problem with her earring.

5 a Helen   c Hazel's children
b Hazel   d No

2

1 T.10.2.

a cheque book   e boyfriend
b birthday cake f chewing gum
c phone number   g policeman
d armchair   h orange juice

2 first

4 a wine bar   e living room
    concert hall   bathroom
    nightclub   dining room
b suitcase   bedroom
    handbag   f post office
    briefcase   newsagent's
c postcard   clothes shop
    credit card   book shop
    birthday card g schoolteacher
    phone card   businessman
d dishwasher   policeman
    video recorder   hairdresser
    word processor   shop assistant
    washing machine

3

1 Canada: Montreal   Ottawa (c)

New Zealand: Auckland
    Wellington (c)

The United Kingdom:
    Birmingham   Liverpool
    London (c)

The United States: Los Angeles
    New York   Washington (c)

2 T.10.3.A.

a In area, Canada is the largest.
    The USA is bigger than
    Australia.

b The UK is smaller than New
    Zealand in area.

c New Zealand has the smallest
    population.

d Birmingham is bigger than
    Liverpool.

e New York is the oldest.

f London has a larger population
    than Los Angeles.

g New York has a larger
    population than New Zealand.

UNIT 11

1

1 T.11.1.B.

day
nine
boy
now
no / know
hair
hear / here
tour

3 a 7   b 4   c 2   d 6
    e 1   f 5   g 3

T.11.1.C.

1. a cold nose
2. fair hair
3. a loud shout
4. a lazy day
5. a bright light
6. noisy boys
7. a real beard

2

3 a true   d false
    b false   e false
    c true   f false

T.11.2.B.

a. In number 1, there are a lot
    of fans.
b. Someone rang in number 3.
c. There's a bang in number 8.
d. The man in number 9 is wrong.
e. Number 14 is 'thin'.
f. There's a tongue in number 15.

3

1 T.11.3.A.

a I've got two children.
b I'll have a coffee, please.
c She's nineteen years old.
d I'm very hungry.
e I'd like two cokes, please.
f They're over there.
g No, they aren't Spanish –
    they're from Argentina.
h He's got a headache.

2 a ✓   b ✗   c ✓   d ✓
    e ✗   f ✓   g ✗   h ✓

UNIT 12

1

2 Dover – Jo
    Boston – John
    born in York – George
    water – George
    Coca-Cola – Jo
    coffee – John
    polo – Jo
    golf and hockey – John
    all sports – George
    smokes – Jo
    talks – George
    a lot of chocolate – John

T.12.1.B.

John
John's from Boston. He drinks
coffee and plays golf and hockey.
He eats a lot of chocolate.

George
George is from York. He drinks
water and likes all sports. He talks
and talks and talks and talks ...

Jo
Jo comes from Dover. She loves
Coca-Cola, and her favourite sport
is polo. She smokes a lot.

3

1 T.12.3.A.

a I'm going out to buy a
    newspaper.
b They're waiting to see the
    manager.
c My daughter's studying to
    become a doctor.
d My brother's going abroad to
    work.
e We're going to the airport to
    meet some friends.
f She's getting ready to go out
    with her boyfriend.

2 weak

3 T.12.3.B.

D Where are you going, Dad?
F To the station to meet Mum.
D Oh, what time's her train?
F Twenty to five. Do you want to
    come?
D No, I've got to go to the doctor's
    at quarter to five.
F Oh, yes, well, see you later!
D See you!

4

1 1A dance   4A go home
    2A garden   5A party
    3A drink   6A washing-up

2 1 ✓   2 ✗   3 ✓   4 ✗   5 ✓   6 ✗

4 a Let's play a game!
    b Shall we do some writing now?
    c Let's have a break!
    d Shall we go out for coffee?
    e Let's have a test next week!
    f Shall we have a class party?

UNIT 13

1

2 T.13.1.B.

main let get sail

4 Last year, I went to Spain on holiday with my friend Jane. The hotel was great, but the weather was terrible! It rained every day for ten days!

5 a An African elephant weighs ten tonnes.
   b Elvis Presley played jazz.
   c The train from Newcastle to London takes eight hours.
   d Laurel and Hardy met in the USA in 1928.
   e Julie read about the weather in Liverpool.

6 T.13.1.D.
   a An African elephant weighs five to seven tonnes.
   b Elvis Presley played rock 'n' roll.
   c The train from Newcastle to London takes four hours.
   d Laurel and Hardy met in the USA in 1926.
   e Julie read about the weather in Budapest.

2

1 /ʃ/ is also spelt s, ci and ti in the examples.

2 6
   Sheila is a receptionist at the International Hotel in Chicago. At the moment she's studying Spanish.

5 a Spanish beach
      some Scottish children
      a Frenchman eating cheese
      two Chinese men playing chess
      Sheila catching a fish
      an English teacher
      a pair of cheap shoes

3

1 a a   e io   i e
   b o   f io   j ou
   c e   g u
   d ia   h a

---

3 a German   Mexican
   b London   pardon
   c listen   garden
   d optician   beautician
   e decision   revision
   f station   pronunciation
   g successful   careful
   h arrival   hospital
   i parent   student
   j delicious   famous

4

2 a adj   e adj
   b adj   f adj
   c both   g both
   d adv   h adv

3 T.13.4.
   a What a fantastic idea!
   b It was an easy exam.
   c The weather was absolutely awful!
   d He got into their office easily.
   e She speaks excellent English and Italian.
   f It was an incredible experience!
   g She lives in a really attractive area.
   h I'll phone for an ambulance immediately.

4 A ends in a consonant sound;
   B begins with a vowel sound.

5 b It was an easy exam.
   c The weather was absolutely awful!
   d He got into their office easily.
   e She speaks excellent English and Italian.
   f It was an incredible experience!
   g She lives in a really attractive area.
   h I'll phone for an ambulance immediately.

6 like a   single or   return or
   this evening   change and

1

3 a /tʃ/   e /dʒ/   i /dʒ/
   b /j/   f /tʃ/   j /dʒ/
   c /tʃ/   g /j/
   d /j/   h /dʒ/

4 a /j/ yoga, yacht, yoghurt
   b 1. /dʒ/ jacket, jeans
      2. /dʒ/ gin, geography
   c /tʃ/ chocolate, chimpanzee, chess

2

2

1 leave	2 where	3 this
4 won't	5 were	6 want
7 hungry	8 work	9 walk
10 live	11 angry	12 these

T.14.2.B.
A Right, so we've got twelve boxes ...
B Yeah.
A ... and twelve words.
B Right.
A ... and I've got to put the right word in each box.
B That's it.
A Ok, so tell me, what's number one?
B Number one is ... *leave* ... that's right, *leave*.
A *Leave* is number one ... OK, so where's *live*?
B That's... er ... number ten.
A *Live* is number ten, OK. And *want* and *won't*, where are they?
B Well, *want* is number six ...
A Number six *want*, yeah.
B ... and *won't* is number four.
A OK ... what else is there ... ah yes, *this*, where's *this*?
B *This* is number three ...
A Yeah.
B ... and *these* is number twelve.
A *These* is number twelve. OK, so what's number two then?
B Number two is *where*.
A *Where* is number two ... right, so what else ...
B Well, number eight is *work*.
A *Work* is number eight, yeah?
B And number nine is *walk*.

A *Work* and *walk*, eight and nine.
OK, which leaves … ah yes,
hungry and *angry* …

B Oh right, yes, so… *hungry* is
number seven …

A Number seven *hungry*, right …

B … and *angry* is number eleven,
at the bottom.

A And that's it …

B No, no … one more … *were*.

A Ah yes, *were* … so that must be
number five, yes?

B That's it … *were* is number five.
Yes.

A And that's it!

3

1 The correct sentences are:
1. a   5. a
2. b   6. a
3. b   7. b
4. a   8. b

4

have or *has*	✓✓✓✓
've or *'s*	✓✓✓✓✓✓
haven't or *hasn't*	✓✓

T.14.3.C.

G Hello, Henry!

H George! How are you?

G Fine! We've just come back
from our holiday!

H Yes?

G Yes! We've been to Italy! Have
you been there?

H Oh, yes, I have. I've been to
Italy many, many times.

G Oh.

H I've seen the Colosseum.

G Oh.

H I've been in a gondola.

G Oh.

H **And** I've climbed the Tower of
Pisa.

G Oh.

H Twice.

G Oh, no, we haven't done any of
those things.

H No.

G But we have seen the Pope!
Have you seen him?

H Er, no, I haven't.

G Ah!

H But my wife has.

UNIT 15

1

1 The **correctly** stressed words are:

1. b   2. b   3. b   4. a
5. b   6. a   7. b   8. b
9. b   10. b   11. a   12. a

2

      /ə/ ●
2. afternoon

      /ə/ ●
3. cassette

     ● /ə/
6. dictionary

     /ə/●
8. Japan

     /ə/● /ə/ /ə/
9. photographer

     /ə/● /ə/
10. policeman

     ● /ə/
12. vegetable

4, 5, 7, and 11 have no /ə/ sound.

3 a ✓ b ✗ c ✗
  d ✗ e ✗ f ✓

2

3 I know you've never liked Martin.
You didn't want me to go out with
him because you said he was just a
car salesman and he wasn't good
enough for me. I know that you've
always wanted the best for me, but
Martin is best for me. I love him
very much indeed.

3

1 **Activity 1**

a table chair cat carpet

b tea orange juice coffee train

c nurse secretary flower
  businessman

d school bread shop church

e football tennis skiing talking

Activity 2

don't   /dəʊnt/
won't   /wəʊnt/
can't   /kɑːnt/
weren't   /wɜːnt/
doesn't   /dʌzənt/

Activity 3

a 3 Paul's taller than George.

b 5 Did you finish your fish and
    chips?

c 2 There's another thing.

d 4 Your son's just rung up.

e 3 What's the first word you
    heard?

f 3 John's got yoghurt on his
    jacket and jeans.

Activity 4

Bill and Lynn
Dave and Jane
Frank and Ann
Steve and Jean
Eddie and Wendy

Activity 5

This is a secret message. If you
know all the phonemic symbols
you don't need to study page fifty
again.

Phonemic symbols

The correct words from the box
for the symbols on page 50 are as
follows:

1	pencil	23	jeans
2	bag	24	sing
3	ticket	25	tea
4	door	26	is
5	key	27	bed
6	Greece	28	hand
7	five	29	start
8	vocabulary	30	not
9	sit	31	your
10	lives	32	good
11	like	33	do
12	man	34	love
13	no	35	girl
14	hot	36	sister
15	read	37	day
16	we	38	go
17	yellow	39	why
18	three	40	down
19	that	41	noise
20	shoe	42	beer
21	television	43	hair
22	choose	44	tour

Oxford University Press
Walton Street, Oxford OX2 6DP

Oxford New York
Athens Auckland Bangkok Bombay
Calcutta Cape Town Dar es Salaam Delhi
Florence Hong Kong Istanbul Karachi
Kuala Lumpur Madras Madrid Melbourne
Mexico City Nairobi Paris Singapore
Taipei Tokyo Toronto
and associated companies in
Berlin Ibadan

OXFORD and OXFORD ENGLISH
are trade marks of Oxford University Press

ISBN 0 19 433940 8

© Oxford University Press 1996

The authors would like to acknowledge their debt to the writers of
various standard pronunciation reference books, especially Ann Baker
Introducing English Pronunciation, A. C. Gimson *A Practical Course
of English Pronunciation*, Joanne Kenworthy *Teaching English
Pronunciation*, Colin Mortimer *Elements of Pronunciation*, and
P. Roach *English Phonetics and Phonology*.

Cartoon illustrations by Nicki Elson, Gordon Lawson, and Nigel Paige.

Designed by Holdsworth Associates, Isle of Wight
Printed in Malta by Interprint Limited